"Roberta once again gives us a smart, sensible approach—filled with practical ideas and tips—to win the war for talent. Without a plan for developing and growing your talent, you will spend countless resources and money on recruiting and hiring—only to see them walk out the door soon after. Thank you, Roberta, for a clear plan for growing our talent!

—Sandy Rezendes, head of strategic onboarding,
Citizens Bank

EVERGREEN
TALENT

A Guide to
Hiring and Cultivating
a Sustainable Workforce

Roberta Chinsky Matuson

CAREER
PRESS

This edition first published in 2020 by Career Press, an imprint of
Red Wheel/Weiser, LLC
With offices at:
65 Parker Street, Suite 7
Newburyport, MA 01950
www.redwheelweiser.com
www.careerpress.com

ISBN: 978-1-63265-161-7
Library of Congress Cataloging-in-Publication Data
available upon request

Cover design by Kathryn Sky-Peck
Cover illustration by iStock
Interior by Scriptorium Book Packagers
Typeset in Minion Pro and Frutiger

Printed in Canada
MAR
10 9 8 7 6 5 4 3 2 1

This book is dedicated to my husband, Ron, whose love and support for me is evergreen. When other spouses may have said, "No way, not another book!" you said, "Why not?"

I also dedicate this book to my children, Zach and Alexis, who are standing tall every day as they make their way through college. Finally, to my parents, Sy and Jeanette Chinsky, and to my sister Debby McClain, who always supported me. And to my brother, Mark Chinsky, for, without his tech talent, this book may never have been finished.

Acknowledgments

I t takes a village to get a book published, and I'm fortunate to have lots of great people in mine. First, my agent Linda Konner, whose belief in me pushes me to pursue the next book. Her tenacity ensures that someone is actually reading what I'm writing. Thank you to my editor Michael Pye, who eagerly agreed to publish this book, and to the whole team at Career Press. A big thank you goes to Tanya Savas, who helped me immensely behind the scenes.

My deepest gratitude goes to my mentor Alan Weiss, who keeps challenging me to think big and encourages me to share my thought leadership with others. I'm slowly catching up to him in terms of the number of books written!

Thanks to all my clients who have entrusted me with their businesses. It's a responsibility I don't take lightly.

Finally, thanks to my friends and colleagues who have been with me throughout this process and have pushed me to continue to soar: Noah Fleming, Hugh Blane, Gail Bower, Marlene Chism, Graham Binks, Dorie Clark, Linda Popky, Simma Lieberman, and Lisa McLeod.

Contents

Part II: Seeding Your Organization

Part III: Cultivating Your Workforce

Introduction

In my life, I've been fortunate to have traveled around the world. As you might imagine, my adventures allowed me to see some truly amazing things. However, nothing could have prepared me for the experience of walking through the majestic Muir Woods National Monument, located north of San Francisco— redwoods standing tall, with their crowns stretching to reach the brilliant sun and the misty coastal fog.

It's easy to get lost in thought as you meander through the forest. I remember thinking, "These trees have been here forever." In doing some research, I discovered that a handful of these breathtaking trees may have grown from a seed that's only roughly the same size as the seed of a tiny tomato plant! However, the majority of redwoods grow most successfully from sprouts that form around the base of a mature tree, utilizing the existing nutrients and root system of the older tree. In ideal conditions, a coastal redwood can grow two or three feet in height annually. But when the trees are stressed from lack of moisture and sunlight, they could grow as little as one inch per year. As I walked through the forest, I realized that the secret to creating, growing, and sustaining an organization filled with world-class talent was rooted right beneath my feet. We'll call this "evergreen talent."

You see, we tend to look at organizations that appear grand— just like the Muir Forest—and forget that they too started out as nothing more than a bunch of seedlings. Somewhere along the way, the leader searched for the right people to plant in the organization. The leader made sure the conditions were fertile for growth. Care and attention were given to new hires to ensure they thrived where they were planted. As the workforce matured, other successful employees sprouted and flourished under the guidance of seasoned veterans. Collaborations between new and experienced talent grew a prosperous, vibrant organization at every level.

As a consultant, I have witnessed similar growth patterns with my best clients. I've worked with hundreds of organizations ranging in size from Fortune 100 companies—like General Motors and Microsoft—to midsize and emerging businesses whose names you haven't heard of (at least, not yet!). All of these organizations have one thing in common: They need talented people to run their businesses. Nowadays, the biggest challenge my clients face is attracting talent that will stick around.

I find myself consistently pondering the same question: How is it that some companies appear to effortlessly hire and retain people, while other companies seem to be in a constant state of hiring because they can't fill positions or their people leave so soon after they arrived?

Having worked across all industries, I'm in a unique position to answer this question. Most companies say their employees are their greatest assets, but that line is about as old as the tallest redwood in the Muir Forest! When you dig past the surface, you see where these organizations fall short. Many companies invest a ton of money into building sustainable relationships with their customers, yet fail to do the same with their employees.

World-class companies treat their employees as well as they treat their best customers. They take the time to nurture relationships with prospective employees before needing to add to their headcount, and they continuously work to strengthen their bond with current employees. As a result, the company reputation of these organizations—also known as "employer brand"—is as strong as some of the world's top-selling consumer products.

To achieve similar results within your organization, you'll most likely need to do some clear-cutting. I'm talking about weeding out the excuses that choke even the best-intentioned companies. Rationalizations run rampant throughout organizations and serve as justification for having a less than exceptional workforce. It's not uncommon to hear:

- **Everyone in our industry is having a difficult time finding and keeping people.** I can assure you, someone in your industry has the lion's share of talent. That someone might not be you—just yet.

- **It's the job of HR to hire and develop people.** Actually, it's the job of the hiring manager to recruit and develop team members.

- **People are lucky to have a job with us.** That may have been true during the recession. However, current record levels of low unemployment render this argument inaccurate.

You have to stop buying into these myths, which I'll deconstruct in more detail later—that is, if you want to stand tall and have others look up to your organization in admiration.

Throughout *Evergreen Talent,* I share a host of stories and ideas from diverse industries and companies of all sizes. At first glance, some of these suggestions could seem much grander than what you think you need or can handle. I implore you not to rush to judgment. Be open to all possibilities. The talent landscape has changed dramatically throughout the past five years. It makes sense that you will need to significantly change your approach to hiring and retaining talent as well. In this book, I'll show you how.

I've included exercises, such as self-assessments, to help you apply the learning to your particular situation. Record your answers/responses on your computer or in a notebook or journal, as no doubt you'll want to refer back to them from time to time.

Let's get growing!

I

Preparing Your Organization for Perpetual Growth

1.

Debunking the Myth:
Talent Will Grow Where It's Planted

Let me share with you what I see organizations doing left and right in regards to talent. Companies are shoveling a ton of time and money into talent management programs, without any consideration of the conditions necessary for this talent to take root. If this is your approach, let me suggest you dig a big hole and throw in a wad of cash. At least you'll know where your money went!

Countless organizations are laboring under the misconception that people will grow wherever they are planted. If that were true, then why are so many employees dying on the vine? Just like the redwood trees, the conditions must be right for optimal employee growth and production. But before we go any further, let me define what I mean by "talent."

Talent Defined

I define "talent" as an aptitude or skill that allows someone to do something particularly well. Lots of people think that talent is something you're either born with or you're not. With certain talents—like the ability to compete at an Olympic level or sing at The Met—this may be true. However, in most cases, it's my belief that talent can be developed.

Employers today are in desperate need of talent—and this isn't limited to the open positions in an organization that need to be filled. Executives would like to believe their workplaces are overflowing with exceptional workers. However, this is rarely the case. Here's an example of what I mean when I say that talent is in short supply.

In my job as a consultant, I'm often asked to work with the senior leadership team to assess talent. As part of this process, I take the team through an exercise I like to call "Next Stop, Growth." This exercise begins with a discussion about the future state of the organization. I ask the leadership team questions like, "Where is the organization heading in the next year or two? How will things be different as a result of this shift? What skills will people need to be successful in this new environment?"

Once we get clear on the destination and what we'll need in terms of talent, the next step is preparation for the upcoming expedition. A great deal of time is spent answering the questions, "Who will be going with us on our new journey, and who should disembark here?"

This is where the rubber hits the road. When asked to think critically and strategically about the future of their organization, it begins to dawn on the leadership team that the talent they thought they had really isn't all that spectacular. Executives immediately start discussing plans to move mediocre employees out to make room for their dream team.

It can be exciting as leaders begin to fantasize about the kind of talent they want, as opposed to what they currently have. The reality behind this fantasy is that executive teams will need to determine which of their existing employees simply don't have the potential to grow, in contrast with those employees who have been stunted by existing management practices, styles, or personality types. It's very important for leaders to be able to recognize the difference between these two types of employee if they want to grow an evergreen workforce. One of these types of employee needs to be let go to make room for new saplings to take root. The other type of employee is worth keeping around and investing resources into their development. Let me give you an example of the difference between the two from my days in the trenches.

A Story from the Trenches: From Near Death to Difference-Maker of the Year

Early in my career, I was offered a position with a financial services consulting firm to develop their human resources department. I was excited by the opportunity, and most important, I really liked the woman who would be my manager. She seemed fully committed to providing me with the resources and support needed to be successful in this newly established role.

Things went quite well during my first few weeks on the job. My boss seemed pleased with my work, and I couldn't have been happier. Little did I know, this was about to change.

One afternoon, my boss came to me and said she was leaving the firm. I sat there in disbelief. If you've ever experienced what it's like to be hired by someone who departs so soon after your first day, then you know how I felt. I was nervous. What if the person who replaced her wasn't nearly as supportive as my current boss? I tried to tell myself I was worried for no reason. Alas, that wasn't the case.

My new boss was a tyrant. Nothing I did pleased her. I went from extremely competent to completely inept overnight. I did everything humanly possible to make my new boss happy. And I almost died trying. I lasted just over a year; I left feeling defeated and depleted.

My next job was head of HR for an overnight delivery service. Again, I was hired to build out the organization's HR department. My boss gave me the freedom to do my job. He complimented me often, and he gave me the support and resources I needed to be successful in my role. I got more done during my first year than anyone expected, and with no staff to speak of.

Like many companies, the organization I worked for held an annual offsite management meeting where they celebrated the successes of the year. I was in on the planning because the event included recognizing members of the management team who had gone above and beyond the call of duty. The evening of the employee recognition dinner is one that I will never forget. After the awards had been given out, the CEO informed the team that there was one award remaining. He called this the Difference-Maker of the Year Award. The CEO explained that this award was for the person whose work had the most significant impact on the organization. Imagine my surprise when my name was called! I thought, "How could this be?" I had no idea there was even such an honor— and *I* was the recipient!

At that moment, I realized the irony of my award. In a year's time, I had gone from having a near-death experience with my former employer to being the most valued employee of the year at my new organization. Yet nothing about *me* had changed. I hadn't gained more experience in my field, nor had I taken any courses that would have contributed to improving my performance. There were only two differentiating factors: my boss and the company that employed me. My new organization had provided me with the right climate for growth, and in that climate, my talent blossomed.

How Leaders Stunt Employee Growth

My story is an example of the impact leaders have on their people. With that in mind, let's look at how leaders inadvertently stunt employee growth. In the interest of space, we'll limit this discussion to the six most common occurrences.

1. Lack of sunlight. Managers that hover over their employees have a huge impact on employee productivity, morale, and growth. This unhealthy condition is also commonly referred to as "micromanagement." Researchers from the University of Birmingham Business School recently studied two years worth of data on 20,000 workers to determine the effects of autonomy on employee morale and well-being.[1] Generally, this study demonstrated that higher levels of autonomy experienced by a worker correlated with a higher sense of job satisfaction and well-being.

This research is consistent with my own findings as a consultant and as a former employee. Employees want to feel in control. They want to be able to make decisions for themselves, contribute their ideas, and operate with limited supervision. If your people are unable to do this, then how can they grow?

If this is sounding familiar, you might suffer from a lack of sunlight as well. Employees thrive on growth, and you probably want the same. It's my experience that when employees don't get what they need, they tend to leave.

2. Wrong species for your climate. Everyone wants to hire the best and the brightest. If you're successful in doing so, will these employees thrive in your organization's climate?

I have a client in the beverage industry who used to recruit salespeople at several well-known universities. Occasionally, their recruiting efforts paid off, but not for long. Without question, and always within a year's time, the hires from these prestigious schools would move on to bigger and better opportunities. When I asked former employees why they left, they'd tell me things like, "The job wasn't stimulating enough," or "The company doesn't quite know what to do with people like me."

It's interesting to note that recruits from less big name schools tended to remain with the company. Furthermore, these employees seemed quite satisfied. That's because they were the right species of talent for the organization, and the conditions were ideal for their growth.

3. Underutilization. If you've ever worked for a company at which people are permitted to stay regardless of performance, then you've most likely experienced what it's like to be underutilized. You do a great job at work, and you're ready for a promotion. Only there is no place for you to go. This is probably because the company vines haven't been pruned in years.

Effective leaders are constantly assessing their workforces and adjusting as they go along. They are not afraid to counsel and eliminate weak links in the organization because they know that pruning will allow other branches in the organization to thrive. If you suspect employees are being underutilized, then perhaps it's time to remove people who are simply taking up space. This is often what is needed to make room for new seedlings to grow.

4. Insufficient tools to get the job done. Several years ago, a friend and I took our teenagers to lunch at a restaurant on Cape Cod during the height of the season. We got there early, and we happened to be the first people seated. You can imagine our surprise when the hostess handed us four menus for six people. When we asked for two additional menus, the hostess explained that they didn't have any more. This woman was trying to do her job, but she wasn't given the tools to succeed!

Employees need the right tools to get their work done. When a leader doesn't provide an appropriate and well-stocked toolbox, the end result is frustration. If you want your employees to improve, then provide them with the tools to do so. This includes training and development, which we'll discuss further in Chapter 8.

5. Lack of nutrients in the soil. The soil at my house is mostly clay: It isn't ideal for growing much except weeds. I learned a long time ago that if I wanted a garden or even grass, I'd have to add nutrients to the soil. Some summers I forget—and when I do, brown patches appear on my lawn, and my plantings barely grow. But when I remember to put down fertilizer, my property could be a contender for best-looking lawn on the street.

I've noticed a similar phenomenon in organizations. The companies that consistently make an effort to add nutrients to their corporate culture fare best. Examples of this include: new initiatives to recognize employee performance; innovative benefits to meet the needs of a diverse workforce; the introduction of new technology to help employees do their jobs more efficiently; the addition of exciting company events and trainings; or a reinvigorated corporate mission to keep employees engaged in their work.

6. Failure to tend to your bed of talent. I can rattle off a list of companies that used to have the reputation of being great employers to work for. If you scored a job with one of these organizations, you never left. Sadly, a number of these companies no longer exist.

One such company is the former retailer Circuit City. If you wanted to work in retail sales, Circuit City was the place to be. Then one day, the company forgot what made their stores so much better than the competition. To save money, they stopped paying commissions to their salesforce. Then, they fired 3,400 of their most experienced salespeople. Crazy, right? Many of Circuit City's top salespeople went to work for the competition, who welcomed them with open arms. It probably won't surprise you to learn that the competition is still in business, and is continuing to thrive and grow.

The lesson for leaders is to take care of the people who make your organization special; without them, you may go the way of Circuit City. Pay your best employees based on results, acknowledge them for their efforts, and provide them with career paths so they choose to remain with your organization for the long haul.

Why Talent Is in Demand in Any Economy

As of this writing, the economy is humming on all cylinders. Business is growing, and new companies are sprouting up daily. It's easy to see why talent is in demand. Companies need people to sell, produce, and deliver their products and services. Although there's been much talk of robots replacing humans, that day is as far away as the next galaxy.

But what happens when business begins to slow down? Does this mean you no longer need great people? Should that scenario occur, strong team members become more important than ever.

Suppose you have to lay off a portion of your workforce to get through a slow period. You'll need to have a core foundation of outstanding employees on hand—people who are capable of taking on the extra work that laid off employees were carrying. Mediocre employees won't be able to handle the load.

As you can see, talent never goes out of style. Keep this in mind, and you'll be well positioned to weather any storm that may come your way.

Applying the Knowledge

Here are some questions to think about as you examine the current state of the workplace in your organization.

- ¤ How often do you hire people, only to ignore them once they're on board? When you do this, what opportunities are you missing? What can be done differently in your organization to prevent "hire and ignore" practices from occurring?

¤   Do you have a lot of talent in your organization, or might you be mistaken? What metrics are you using to assess the talent you think you have?

¤   How quickly do you weed people out of your organization after realizing they are no longer suited for your company's climate? What steps can you take to avoid being in this situation in the first place? What are you willing to do to accelerate the process of transitioning out the dead weight?

¤   What are you personally guilty of in terms of stunting employee growth? Which area are you willing to work on first, so that you can change this dynamic?

¤   What's your commitment level to growing talent? What barriers need to be removed to achieve your goals? How willing are you to hold managers accountable for the development of their people?

2.

Surveying the Terrain:
The Five Essential Elements Needed
for Evergreen Talent

I'm going to share with you a phenomenon I've observed that I'm sure you've noticed as well. Some people who are highly successful in their roles somehow fail miserably when they take a similar position in a new environment. Have you ever wondered why this happens? I've coached some very well-regarded professionals who have found themselves in this exact situation after moving to a new organization, so I've thought about this question a lot.

What I have found is that the conditions have to be right for people to thrive. No matter how skilled employees may be, they'll never succeed if the environment isn't a good fit for them. Think carefully about the types of people who will flourish best in *your* organization, and you'll be able to avoid costly mis-hires!

Let me give you an example of what I mean when I say that conditions must be well suited for the kinds of workers you are hiring. Sustaining talent and business growth in a law firm requires very different conditions than those conditions needed to sustain and grow talent in a tech firm. You might notice when you are researching a law firm to handle your company's legal matters that the attorney bios are often filled with words like "Mr. Doe has spent the last twenty years with our firm." Mr. Doe may be pictured wearing a suit, sitting in front of a gray or navy backdrop. In contrast, you've probably seen your friends in the start-up sector happily announcing their new jobs once every six to eighteen months on LinkedIn (note: this isn't always a bad thing). While researching your colleague's new company, you could stumble across a fun-looking montage of her in front of a green screen in various poses! The species of employee who is happy sitting behind the same mahogany desk for twenty years probably won't be happy when you ask him to switch roles once every quarter—and vice versa. Why? Because those who will prosper and remain happily employed in a service firm are a different species of employee than those who gravitate to a start-up.

Once business leaders have a thorough understanding of their own terrain, as well as the outside elements impacting their environment, they'll be poised to create the ideal conditions for evergreen talent to prosper in *their* organization.

Before we go further, take a few minutes and think about where your company is currently at in terms of talent. I've created the following assessment to help you gain a clear understanding of your current state so you can focus on those areas with the most growth opportunity for you.

Please rate your company in each of the following areas in the chart on pages 19 and 20 using the rating system below:

4 = All of the time

3 = Most of the time

2 = Sometimes

1 = Rarely

0 = Never

N/A = Not applicable

ATTRACTION	
We have a pool of well-qualified candidates waiting to come work for us.	
There are more qualified applicants than we can process.	
The people who apply are a good fit.	
When we invite candidates in for an interview, they say yes.	
Our top-choice candidates accept our job offers.	
Employees regularly refer friends and colleagues to our company.	
People outside the company regularly recommend top people to our organization.	
We have a strong reputation for being a great place to work.	
We screen candidates in, rather than screening candidates out.	
We are able to fill job openings without the help of recruitment agencies and search firms.	
RETENTION	
Our top employees choose to stay with our firm.	
Employees consider our company a great place to work.	
We regularly invest in the development of our people.	
We hold managers responsible for employee turnover in their areas.	

We know who our top performers are, and we support their growth.	
Employees would rate their managers as being great to work for.	
Our managers are trained to select, identify, guide, coach, reward, and retain their people.	
Employees know exactly what is expected of them, and they have the tools and skills to perform their jobs satisfactorily.	
Employees feel they are compensated fairly for their contribution to our company.	
We regularly ask our employees what we can do to improve our workplace.	

Any area with a score of 2 or less requires immediate attention!

In my work as a consultant for organizations ranging from Fortune 500 companies to 10-person start-ups, I have identified five essential elements that are necessary for evergreen talent in *any* organization:

1. Ideal climate
2. Commitment
3. Nutrients
4. Leadership
5. Implementation

This chapter will look at these necessary preconditions for evergreen talent and illustrate how you can put them into action within your own organization. Remember, the way you apply the five necessities for evergreen talent will depend on the specific type of organization you are working in.

Ideal Climate

Let's begin with the climate in an organization, which has a huge impact on both talent and business growth. You can also think about climate as the company culture. I like to use my mentor Alan Weiss's definition of "culture," which is "a shared set of beliefs and values." A company's culture sets the stage for how work gets carried out within an organization. This includes work schedules, everyday management, how communication takes place, and acceptable behavior.

People need to understand that most organizations have subcultures. Visit a website like Glassdoor, and you'll find employees writing reviews about their experiences working for a particular employer. Some employees tout how wonderful it is to work for their employer, while simultaneously, others warn people to stay away! In all likelihood, the people praising their employer work in a particular department or area of the company where each day is a sunny day. Others work under some pretty gloomy, gray conditions.

This raises the question: How can companies establish a more consistent climate throughout their organizations? The answer is twofold. First, you must hire and develop strong leaders. With the proper care and attention, most people can mature into strong leaders (I will provide guidance on how you can grow your own crop of stellar leaders later in Chapter 11). Then, you have to give these leaders the authority and autonomy to do their jobs. Keep in mind that the latter part is just as important as the first part of this equation.

The majority of companies have established policies and procedures that govern how work is done. However, most of these policies were written years ago—and many no longer make sense. Yet managers are still held to these often arbitrary standards, which means leaders do not have the freedom to operate under the one rule that really matters: the rule of common sense. For leaders who are innovators, this can be extremely frustrating. *Nothing halts innovation faster than bureaucracy.* Keep in mind that the reason companies hire innovative leaders is because they *want* people who can think out of the box . . . at least, that's what they say they want.

Be very clear on what the climate is *really* like in your organization so that you can hire people who will fit in and prosper. If there is a lot of process and protocol required to get anything done, prospective employees need to know this. Likewise, if rules are off the table in the face of innovation, job candidates should be informed of this.

These days, it may seem like you have to be a hip company that closely resembles a start-up, or you won't attract people. That's not true. Not everyone wants to spend their evenings at work eating dinner out of a cardboard box because their company is racing to be the next breakthrough tech company. Take the time to clearly define your company culture, and then remain true to that definition in practice. By doing so, you'll attract the *right* talent for your company—which in the end, is all that really matters.

I regularly work with clients to help them define their company culture. While the entire process could easily be the subject of another book, here's a brief preview of some of the questions that I ask. This will help you start to develop a succinct company culture definition.

- ☒ Why does our company exist?
- ☒ What do we believe?
- ☒ What are our core values?
- ☒ What is our vision for the company?

People want to know where they are going and why they are doing the work they are doing. A well-defined culture provides your employees with answers to these important questions.

Here are some additional questions to think about when trying to determine the type of employee who will thrive, given your climate zone.

- ☒ What characteristics do the most successful people in your organization have in common?
- ☒ What traits did those who have been unsuccessful in your organization share?
- ☒ What does it take to succeed in a company like yours?
- ☒ What would employees say are the top three reasons they love working in your company? (Don't know? Ask!)
- ☒ How would *you* describe your company? (Note: this is *not* about the company line that your PR department has crafted.)

Commitment

Your efforts to create evergreen talent will tank without commitment. Your leaders need to be fully committed to creating evergreen talent. For many, this will be a huge shift. Lots of managers are happy having HR people take responsibility for work that they don't want to do. By keeping distant from the hiring process, managers can blame HR when jobs go unfilled, when workers aren't properly trained, and when employees don't work out.

However, managers are ultimately responsible for how their departments perform. Giving managers back the responsibility for staffing their departments and training their people will result in a deeper commitment to employees. No doubt you'll see productivity rise, along with profits. Of course, as part of this process, managers must be trained on how to recruit, hire, and develop their work teams. This will take less time, effort, and money than what you are currently spending when jobs go unfilled or employee turnover goes haywire because your managers aren't fully committed to the success of their people.

What should you consider as you get your managers on board with the process?

Focus on what's in it for them. People act based on emotion. Yep, that's right. We are motivated to do something when we feel it's in our best interest to do so. An example of how this works follows.

You are not really in the market for a new car when you and your wife, who happens to be seven months pregnant, pass a car dealership. You pull up in your subcompact and start to walk around the car lot. Within two minutes, a car salesman asks what brought you in today. You tell him you're just looking. He can't help but notice that your spouse is about to have a baby, so he immediately steers you to an SUV that has the highest safety rating and tells you all about the safety features. You begin to have visions of your baby safely in the back seat, happily smiling. Before you know it, you're the new owner of one of the safest cars on the road!

We've all been there. In fact, I drove away in a new SUV with my baby in tow because of acting on emotion. As a side note, it was a good move; several months later we were hit by another vehicle, and no one was hurt!

How can you get your leadership team fully on board? Frame things in a way that clearly explains how much better *their* lives are going to be be once they adopt this new way of acquiring and growing talent.

Change	Outcome
Full autonomy in terms of who they hire	Better and faster hiring decisions
Full responsibility for people decisions in their areas, including employee terminations	Less frustration and more control
Fully staffed department	Better work/life balance

Remind your leaders that those who do a terrific job of developing their people will be the ones who will receive better pay raises and faster promotions.

Reward managers who manage the full life cycle of their teams. Managers are supposedly paid to do this. However, managers are rarely penalized for not filling jobs rapidly enough or for making more bad hires than most. That's understandable. Many organizations run talent acquisition as a separate entity, and as a result, it is difficult to hold leaders accountable. This can no longer be the case.

To effectively measure talent management, organizations need to take three key steps:

1. Determine the right metrics to track.

2. Implement a process to record, track, and report on the core metrics.

3. Develop a process for analyzing and interpreting the metrics.

It's best to include managers when defining the metrics that will be used to measure their performance so they are fully invested in the outcomes. Whatever you decide to measure, make sure these metrics drive business results. Example metrics:

- Number of days jobs go unfilled (also known as time to hire)
- Robustness of talent pipeline
- Cost to hire talent
- New hire retention rate
- Rate of internal promotions
- Next-level readiness
- Production
- Employee turnover (can be broken down into voluntary and involuntary)
- Workforce diversity
- Employee engagement scores
- Satisfaction rating of candidates (to help you determine the true candidate experience)
- Quality of hires

Nutrients

Employees want to be nurtured and developed, and those companies that provide the nutrients employees seek for personal growth are winning the lion's share of talent. What are the nutrients that feed the souls of employees and keep people engaged? A sense of purpose is high on the list for many. Employees today are no longer satisfied merely increasing company profits. They want their work to have meaning. They also want to make the world a better place. That's great news if you are a nonprofit working toward ending world hunger. But how does a company in an industry like the steel business connect with the hearts of their employees?

Many organizations work hand in hand with nonprofits. Worldwide, employees can be found volunteering at nonprofits on a special day designated for volunteerism or on an ongoing basis. Some organizations, such as State Street Bank, go a step further. This company actually hires the population that nonprofits are serving into State Street Bank itself. For the next four years, the company is committed to hiring a thousand Boston students who have been served by one or more of the Workforce Investment Network organizations. This move allows State Street employees to see purpose in action and as a side benefit, State Street is filling its future talent pipeline. That is a winning formula for all!

In addition to the desire for purpose, employees nowadays have become accustomed to growing in a talent bed that is seeded with benefits. No matter how you personally feel about the outrageous perks that companies use to lure talent, you cannot disregard this phenomenon. And you can compete without breaking the bank.

Here are some suggestions:

- Catered lunches on a weekly or monthly basis
- Periodically hiring a private chef to prepare healthy meals for employees to take home to their families
- Breakrooms stocked with *healthy* snacks
- Food Truck Friday, with food trucks that roll into your parking lot and employees can feast on some new treats
- Subsidies for gym memberships
- Wellness stipends for a healthier lifestyle (e.g., running shoes, tennis racquet, yoga gear, juice cleanses, weight management subscription programs, etc.)

⊠ Three-day weekends during the summer months (winter months if you're located in ski country!)

⊠ Flexibility to work from home

⊠ Student loan debt reimbursement

⊠ Subsidizing commuting costs

⊠ Event tickets (with some extra money thrown in to pay the sitter!)

⊠ Pet-friendly office

⊠ Paid time off to volunteer

⊠ Paid sabbaticals

⊠ Travel stipends to encourage workers to get out of the office and gather inspiration from a location other than home

Looking back to the 1980s when these kinds of perks were not the norm, companies had management training programs, and students would flock to the organizations offering these programs. Then the recession hit, and management training programs went the way of 401(k) matches. Though the financial plan match is back, sadly the same cannot be said for management training programs. This is unfortunate, as today's recent grads probably could benefit more from these programs than the previous generation did.

In his book *Academically Adrift: Limited Learning on College Campuses* (University of Chicago Press, 2011), author and New York University sociologist Richard Arum discusses an unprecedented 2011 study. Arum's research followed several thousand undergraduates through four years of college, and the results were startling. Arum found that many students didn't learn the critical thinking, complex reasoning, and written communication skills that are widely assumed to be the core of a college education. These students are graduating without knowing how to sift fact from opinion, make a clear written argument, or objectively review conflicting reports of a situation or event. Yet we take these graduates, plant them in our organizations, and expect them to survive through osmosis. Clearly, *we* are the ones who have a lot to learn!

Today, it's easier than ever to provide employees with training in real time. You can purchase a company subscription to online learning platforms like Lynda.com—also called LinkedIn Learning—which has more than 9,000 courses as of this writing. (Full disclosure: I'm a LinkedIn Learning author with eight courses on their platform.) There are also MOOCs (massive open online courses) such as Coursera, where many courses are free or charge only a minimal fee for those pursuing certificates.

Other ways to offer development opportunities to your employees include putting on lunch and learns, where you have an industry expert present on a particular topic or you host an author who will discuss her latest book. (Note: Some business authors will waive their speaker fee when you commit to purchasing books for all participants.) Some companies have book clubs that meet during lunch or after work. The employer reimburses the cost of the books for those who participate.

If you have the resources to bump it up a notch, consider hiring executive coaches for high-potential employees and leaders who are ready to step up their game. Formal mentoring programs, where mentors are assigned to help mentees navigate through the workplace, can be very effective as well. These and other growth opportunities are discussed in detail in Chapter 8.

Leadership

The key to attracting and retaining talent is great leadership. Employees will transplant themselves rather than get plowed under by a leader who stifles their growth. Talented workers and those with lots of potential won't apply for jobs with companies that have a reputation for poor leadership.

A good place to begin is with an honest evaluation of the leadership in your organization. Take the following assessment. Make note of any rating that is a 2 or below, as these areas require *immediate* attention.

Evergreen Talent Organizational Leadership Self-Assessment

Please rate your company in each of the following areas in the chart on pages 30 and 31 using the rating system below:

4 = All of the time

3 = Most of the time

2 = Sometimes

1 = Rarely

0 = Never

N/A = Not applicable

We know who our top leaders are.	
We support the growth of our top leaders.	
We treat our leaders as assets to invest in, rather than as costs that can be easily reduced.	
We know the *real* reasons employees leave our company, and we use this information to make improvements wherever and whenever possible.	
We take immediate action when a leader has more turnover than most.	
Our leaders receive *continuous* feedback on their performance.	

The people we promote are outstanding leaders.	
Our leaders regularly ask our employees what can be done to improve our workplace.	
Our executives view the attraction and development of talent as a top priority.	
We are satisfied with our employee turnover rates.	
We quickly transition leaders who don't make the grade out of the organization.	
Our customers/clients rave about our employees.	
We are viewed as an exceptional place to work.	
We don't have to go after top talent because they usually approach us.	
Employees understand how their work contributes to the bottom line of the company.	
Employees would rate their managers as being great to work for.	
Our managers are trained to select, identify, guide, coach, reward, and retain their people.	
We provide coaches to our top leaders.	
Employees have the tools and skills to perform their jobs satisfactorily.	
We know how much it costs to replace every employee who leaves the organization.	
I believe that this is a great place to work.	

Five Things to Consider Before Promoting Someone into Management

Leaders promote people into management for a variety of reasons, many of which do not make sense. These reasons range from "She's been with the company the longest" to "We don't have anyone else who understands the software." Sometimes, company management assumes that a top salesperson will automatically be a top leader of the sales department. Rarely is this the case. When this doesn't work out, the organization may wind up losing a great salesperson—plus many of the people who work for that new leader. Consider the following before you promote someone into a leadership position.

1. **Desire.** This comes first, because if someone doesn't really want a leadership role, the rest of the list doesn't matter. Great leadership requires authenticity. You cannot fake enjoying being in a leadership role. You have to really want the job.

2. **Aptitude.** The capacity and readiness to lead others must be scrutinized when promoting people into leadership roles. Younger people are often passed over for leadership roles because of preconceived notions that age is correlated with capability and management readiness, while mature workers are promoted without thoughtful consideration of their aptitude for the job. Think about this before you promote your next employee.

3. **Traits.** The traits or competencies necessary to be successful in a leadership role vary, depending on the level of the position and the industry. Look at your most successful leaders. What traits do they have in common? Does the employee you are considering for promotion possess

similar traits? If not, how difficult will it be for this person to succeed in a management role in your company?

4. **Attitude.** It's not easy coming to work every day with a smile on your face and a can-do attitude when you may be overworked or when business is on a downward trend. Yet, this is exactly what a good leader must do. Does the person you are about to promote have a positive outlook about life in general? If not, take a pass on this person.

5. **Stamina.** Not everyone has the fortitude to be a leader. You have to be willing and able to step in and do the job of others, if they should move on to greener pastures. You must be able to multitask, carry the load, and switch gears at a moment's notice. Low-energy people need not apply.

Implementation

Companies have no problems coming up with ideas. However, many trip up in the execution. Let's take a look at how your company can avoid a similar fate.

Lots of people think they can do everything internally. Like many of you, I started out trying to do everything on my own. After all, isn't that the definition of an entrepreneur? Maybe so, but not a very successful one! After spending five incredibly frustrating hours trying to put together a PowerPoint presentation, it dawned on me that hiring outside help was the smarter use of my time. The old adage still applies: Work smarter not harder. What are you doing internally that could be done more quickly and skillfully by an outside expert?

As you go through this book, pick and choose what areas make the most sense for you to tackle on your own. This will vary from company to company. For example, you may have a team member who does videography and film editing on the side. If that's the case, tap this valuable resource for help in creating videos for employee development or for your employer brand. When it comes to talent strategy, you most definitely will want to partner with an experienced external resource. Why? *Because if you could have done this internally, you would have done so already!*

How to Select and Create Evergreen Partnerships

There are many ways to find evergreen partnerships. In the interest of time and space, let's look at four solid ideas that will help ensure you find the right partner on your first attempt:

1. **Referrals.** My best clients come from referrals. That's because satisfied clients will refer me to like-minded companies. The fit is right, and as a result, we're able to make progress rapidly. This also applies to vendors. Ask people you trust for recommendations, and in all likelihood, they will be more than happy to share their trusted partnerships with you.

2. **LinkedIn.** LinkedIn has become an amazing source for those in need of recommendations. You can post a request for a recommendation for all to see, or you can do so in one of your private groups.

3. **Google.** Search engines can facilitate researching possible alliances. Use them to help you quickly identify who the thought leaders are in a particular area. Then, go to their websites to see if these organizations may be a good fit as possible partners.

4. **Conference attendance.** Talent conferences abound, and if you attend one, you'll hear speakers or meet panelists who may be of service to you. Get cards from prospective partners. Then follow up after the event to determine if you are the right fit for one another.

The key is to select and create evergreen partnerships with experts who can help you build and sustain an outstanding workforce. Once you find these partners and establish strong relationships, chances are you'll be able to tap their networks of other great people. These extended networks can be a fantastic resource to help you in additional areas of your business.

Applying the Knowledge

As you consider the five essential elements required for evergreen talent, ask yourself the following questions in terms of your company.

- ¤ How would you describe the *climate* in your organization? Is this company-wide, or does it vary from department to department? What factors have a daily impact on the climate? What impact, if any, does your corporate climate have on your ability to create an evergreen workforce?

- ¤ What specific steps will you take to ensure a consistent temperature throughout the organization? Which questions will you ask to determine the kinds of people who would thrive in your environment?

- ¤ On a scale of 1–10 (with 10 being high), how committed is your organization when it comes to evergreen talent? If your response is anything less than a 10, what will you do to increase your company's *commitment*? What metrics will you use to measure the commitment levels of your leaders in terms of evergreen talent?

- ¤ What *nutrients* will you add to the soil of your organization to ensure employees are nurtured? How will you fund this? Will employees be involved in selecting additional perks, or will the business owner or someone in corporate determine these benefits?

¤ How did your organization score in terms of *leadership*? What areas did you rate a 2 or below? What steps will you take to improve your scores?

¤ What methodology will you employ to determine if *implementation* can be done in-house or should be outsourced to an expert? What's your plan to find expertise and build partnerships outside your core areas of specialization?

3.

Tilling the Organization: Preparing Your Environment for a New Approach to Talent Cultivation

C hange is difficult for many. However, it's necessary for any business that wants to strive and thrive in our increasingly competitive world. No organization achieves high levels of growth by doing the same things day in and day out while the environment around them is changing. It's simply not possible.

Take the talent landscape. Remember when it was easier to find a hundred-dollar bill on the ground than to find a job? That era was not so long ago. In the past several years, the talent landscape has dramatically changed. Today, employers are giving out hundred-dollar bills (and much more) just to get candidates in the door.

Warnings of a talent tsunami have gone unheeded, resulting in devastation for many. Barren fields of empty cubicles are now a common sight in organizations—particularly for those seeking to staff some of today's more challenging positions, like sales and IT. Nevertheless, leaders continue to operate as if nothing has changed.

The time to make *small* shifts in your talent strategy to achieve results is long gone. What's needed is the evergreen talent approach, where leaders are given full responsibility and are held account- able for the attraction, development, and retention of their people. This responsibility can no longer reside in HR, as HR leaders are having a difficult time managing their *own* talent pipelines.

The Truth About Resistance

Fear and uncertainty fuel resistance. You cannot overcome resistance through force and logic. Many leaders have died trying!

The way to address resistance is by taking an interest in peo- ple's deeply rooted emotions and the needs that drive them. Put your employees' concerns at ease and help them embrace change. Help them to understand how this change will impact them posi- tively. Let's look at some common resistance scenarios you may face when preparing your organization for evergreen talent. I'll also review strategies to overcome these pesky roadblocks.

Five Common Resistance Scenarios and How to Overcome Them

1. **"We've always done it that way!"** If I had an apple for every time I've heard this, I'd have an orchard. Doing things the same way only makes sense if you're consistently getting the results you need. I'm guessing that's not your situation or you wouldn't be reading this book.

Research has repeatedly shown that people are open to change when they view the change as being in their best interests. Your job as the leader is to highlight the *positive* impact this new approach will have for your people. This is easiest when you can show how the change is in your employees' best interests both professionally *and* personally. Ex- amples of what to say to get team members on board are provided. (Note: Of course, only say something if it's true!)

- You'll be able to fill positions more rapidly because you'll no longer have to wait for HR to prescreen resumes.

- You'll have *more* control over who remains on your team and who departs.

- You'll be *recognized and rewarded* for doing a great job of managing your talent pipeline.

- You'll have an opportunity to learn new skills (e.g., how to attract, recruit, and keep A-level players) that will benefit you for years to come.

- Others will look at you as an example of the type of leader they'd like to become.

- When you've fully staffed your team with quality hires, you'll be able to leave the office in time to catch your daughter's soccer games.

- You'll have peace of mind knowing that you've got this, even if someone decides to leave.

2. "Hiring is HR's job." I can't think of a single HR department that's not overwhelmed with everything they've been asked to do. Think about it. In many companies, there's typically one HR employee for every 100 workers. This may not be so bad, if the sole responsibility of HR were staffing and team development. Unfortunately, this is rarely the case. Sure, there may be a team of contract recruiters trying to whittle down the number of openings, but these days, it's still not enough.

According to the July 2019 JOLT's report published by the US Department of Labor, the United States has 7.3 million job openings and an unemployment rate of 3.7%—which means we are pretty much at full employment.[1] Any hiring manager who sits by passively waiting for his HR team to deliver candidates will be waiting a long time! Leaders must pull out all the stops and attract candidates to themselves.

You need to share these startling statistics with your managers and explain why hiring is *not* the job of HR. Then, provide your leaders with guidance as to how to turn their own teams into hiring machines. Expect to hear some pushback like:

3. "I don't have time for this." The correct response to this statement is, "No, actually you do. There's a reason why you are referred to as the *hiring* manager."

I'm not sure exactly when things changed, but somewhere along the way managers, who used to be responsible for hiring and developing team members, were granted permission to delegate this part of their job to other departments. It's time to place this responsibility back where it belongs—with the manager. Let your leaders know what you expect from them in terms of hiring and developing team members. The more specific you can be, the better.

4. "That won't work here." Don't you just hate those words? Of course it will! I know this to be true, because I've implemented what I call the "Evergreen Talent Experience" in a number of diverse organizations. Guess what? Across organizations of varying sizes and in completely different sectors, the Evergreen Talent Experience has been proven to deliver stellar results.

If an employee insists a new approach to talent won't work, my response would be, "You could be right. However, let's give it a try and see what happens." Then redirect the conversation and discuss your plans for implementation.

5. "We won't see immediate results." Yes, this may be true. However, we're looking for long-term results here, not simply one win and then we're done.

Explain to team members that there is no such thing as an overnight success. Tell them that together, you're going to come up with a plan to dramatically improve your ability to attract, develop, and retain talent. You'll course correct along the way.

Why Doing Nothing Is Not an Option

There isn't a person left on the planet who doesn't think the hiring system is broken. Just ask job seekers who've been unsuccessful in connecting with hiring managers, even when they're fully qualified for the position being posted, or the manager who is unable to fill job openings.

If you think labor is in short supply now, just wait. Chances are, it will only get worse. Recruitment is especially challenging for employers in fast-growing sectors, such as health care. Between 2016 and 2026, the Bureau of Labor Statistics anticipates support roles in the health-care industry will increase by 23.6 percent. Job growth is also expected to exceed the national average for financial analysts, accountants, auditors, and IT professionals, among other specialties.[2]

What if you do nothing about the talent situation in your organization right now? Where will you be next year at this time? My guess is that you'll be that much further behind—that is, if your company is still in business. That's because if you're not moving forward, you're falling behind. Work is about to get a lot more stressful for you. Don't let employee resistance prevent you from getting started. Be the exemplar, and eventually, employees will follow your lead.

Here's the good news. The principles I'm sharing in this book don't necessitate an army of people to implement. Choose one or two ideas and move them forward a mile. Then choose a few more. You'll be amazed by how quickly you'll start seeing the results. It's my experience that when people begin to see positive outcomes, they'll quickly jump on board.

Depending on your level of leadership and responsibility in your organization, your ability to take action and your scope of influence may vary. That's okay! You can make a contribution to change at any level. I have written this book so that it can be help-ful to everyone—not just the president or the CEO.

If you're an employee looking to advance your career into management, you can demonstrate the exemplary qualities supe-riors are looking for by embracing and pioneering changes in your organization. You should avoid voicing any of the hesitations listed above at all costs!

If you are a middle manager working within a complex hier-archy, you might have been seeing opportunities for change for what seems like a lifetime. Maybe you can't convince your direct supervisor to support you in the changes that need to be made—yet. As long as you aren't violating the explicit instructions of your manager or the policies of the company, this could be a good time to get creative. Ask your top employees if they'd be willing to take a little extra time to help you pilot a new solution to a problem you've been having in your department. Document your efforts along with the results. Then, approach your supervisor with your findings. Chances are, they'll be a lot more willing to listen when you have hard data in hand.

Lessons from Leaders Who Overcame Resistance

Heidi Pozzo, Founder of Pozzo Consulting and former CFO at Longview Fibre Paper and Packaging, knows all too well what it's like to work in an environment where resistance is deeply rooted in an organization.

Pozzo was hired by a private equity firm to resuscitate a com-pany that was on life support. "When I arrived, people were liter-ally sleeping on the job!" exclaims Pozzo. "Most of the employees had worked their entire careers with this company and were used to doing things a specific way." "We've always done it that way" was the company mantra.

Pozzo worked to overcome resistance by opening up communication throughout the organization. She openly shared information about company finances, and she regularly communicated with team members. Pozzo then focused employees around a common goal that people could understand. She chose safety because this is top of mind for many who work in manufacturing: "We created a visual symbol to remind employees of our goals. Everyone wore a bright safety vest at work, no matter what your position, including me."

Pozzo shared metrics on safety and helped employees understand where they stood in terms of safety in the region and in their industry. Within a few years, the company went from the bottom of the list to close to the top.

Pozzo used this approach to drive change throughout the organization: "We created focus. We got people engaged through the use of work committees and relied on storytelling to spread our message. We showed people we cared and why it was in their best interest to modify their thinking." The results? Pozzo and her team tripled EBITA in four years, which is remarkable by anyone's standards.

In my consulting practice, I help leaders navigate their organizations through change. My client Ronald Bryant, president of Baystate Noble Hospital/Western Region and Baystate Franklin Medical Center/Northern Region, is a master at this. Eight years ago, Bryant was hired to run Noble Hospital and improve the overall health of the organization.

When Bryant arrived, there wasn't much going on in terms of transparency. The leaders mostly thought about themselves and had little regard for the welfare of their employees. Bryant knew he had to make some significant changes in how the organization operated.

"When it comes to change, you have to start somewhere," states Bryant. "You have to ask if the organization is where you want it to be, and if it's not, you have to go about changing it. Otherwise, you are going to be spinning your wheels."

"'This won't work here' is typical in many organizations," notes Bryant, "which makes change initiatives even more challenging." Like Pozzo, Bryant believes you have to empower people to make the changes themselves. To make this happen, Bryant brought transparency to the organization, which allowed him to gain the trust of employees. He then built what he calls an environment of psychological safety. "An employee has to feel it's safe to speak up," explains Bryant. "When they feel secure and that their input matters, they're comfortable saying, 'Hey, maybe there is a better way we can do this.'"

Bryant goes on to say, "You still have to give employees the training to create the opportunities to make the changes because they might not have the skill level, the education, or whatever talents are needed to drive that change."

Bryant was so successful in his efforts to shift the culture and make it more employee and patient centered, that he was asked to replicate these changes at another hospital within the overarching network. Bryant has also been invited to participate in system-wide initiatives, and he is often called upon to share expertise in creating change with others in the organization. A side benefit that Bryant hadn't counted on was getting to see his senior managers, and those below them, expand their roles and have more fulfilling careers.

As you prepare your organization for the shift to evergreen talent, consider the following:

¤ For organizational change to stick, the people in the organization need to be better off as a result of this change. When people understand how they're better off, most will support the change.

¤ Change needs to be driven internally. The people in each part of the organization have to own the change.

¤ You have to show people what good looks like. You can't possibly get an organization to perform better if no one understands the characteristics of world-class performance. People need to see what they are aiming for. Your job as a leader is to show employees where you're all headed in a way they can understand.

¤ Involve people in the process, and provide them with the tools and training they need to create the changes themselves.

Getting a Few Wins Under Your Belt

I recall a time when I attempted to launch a new initiative for my company that I called "Selecting for Success." The purpose of the program was to teach hiring managers how to interview and assess candidates so they would have better hiring outcomes. The plan was to roll the program out to the hiring managers, who resided in eighteen different locations across the Eastern seaboard, over a three-month time period. I thought managers would be thrilled to receive help in this area. That's not exactly how things went.

A large number of managers viewed the development opportunity as one more thing to add to their plates. Some managers were concerned that others would see how inept they really were in terms of interviewing and selecting talent. Some flat-out refused to attend.

I quickly recognized that I had not done a good job of preparing the organization for the change I was getting ready to implement. So I put the plan on hold and recruited several of the company's top influencers to help me pilot this program. I rolled out the program to a few key locations and worked closely with those leaders to support them through the transition. The managers began to experience the benefits of being able to quickly assess and select talent. They shared their successes with their peers. It wasn't long before calls started coming in from other managers, asking me to put their locations next on the list.

I got a few wins under my belt before I took the program company-wide, which enabled me to implement one of the company's most successful initiatives. To my knowledge, the program is still in place.

I learned the hard way that sometimes baby steps are necessary before going all in. If you sense the resistance may be too great to successfully launch your talent initiative, then take a page out of my playbook: Identify a few key influencers in your organization; involve the selected leaders in the development of your program; ask them to be beta testers; have them share their successes with others. Rinse and repeat.

Applying the Knowledge

As you look to evaluate your organization's readiness to grow talent, consider the following questions:

- ¤ How open to change are the people in your organization?

- ¤ What steps can you take to prepare leaders for the shift in the way talent will be managed?

- ¤ What resistance to changing the way talent has always been managed in your organization might you anticipate? How might you respond to this resistance?

- ¤ Think of a time when team members were resistant to a new idea. What did you do to successfully overcome this in the past?

- ¤ Who in the organization is a key influencer? How will you involve key influencers in the planning and rollout of your new talent initiative?

- ¤ How will the change you are planning to implement better the lives of the employees in your organization?

- ¤ How will you present this change to your people to make sure employees are aware of the benefits that are in it for them?

II

Seeding Your Organization

4.

A Matter of Climate:
Identifying the Right Saplings
for Your Environment

Every spring, my husband and I drive to our local nursery and select plantings for our garden. Without fail, I find myself attracted to some flowers that require growing conditions that we simply do not have. Admittedly, some years I'm able to convince my spouse to purchase these beauties anyway, thinking they're way too pretty to pass up. But the results are predictable every time. Halfway through the growing season, we have to get out in the yard and pull a bunch of dead plants. A similar pattern occurs in organizations: Leaders convince themselves that certain candidates will grow and prosper, even though these people are obviously not well suited for the climate in the organization.

I have firsthand experience of what it's like from the employee side of things to be working in an environment that is completely wrong for me. Years ago, I was hired by a firm who should have never made me a job offer. The company was all about pedigree degrees. If you didn't attend a top-tier school, then you may as well not have attended college. The work atmosphere could best be described as elitist.

I wasn't born into a wealthy family, nor did I attend an Ivy League school. I also wasn't comfortable working in a cutthroat environment. Needless to say, the experience was a disaster for me and for my employer. Eventually, I found a work environment more to my liking—and my former employer unearthed someone who was a better fit. However, from what I've been told, it took them a few more rounds to get this right.

Five Common Workplace Cultures and the Talent Best Suited for Each

"Culture," which is defined as a shared set of values and beliefs, varies among workplaces. As a consultant whose work spans across a number of diverse industries, I have a bird's-eye view on how organizations operate, both formally and informally.

I'm going to focus on five common types of culture you're most likely to encounter in the workplace. Then, I'll offer guidance in terms of what variety of talent is best suited for each culture climate. When reading through this list, keep in mind that hybrid cultures exist. Also understand that larger organizations often have distinct subcultures operating simultaneously across separate departments or teams.

Bureaucratic

This type of culture is generally found in hierarchical organizations like government agencies, hospitals, large service firms, and established family businesses. In these types of organizations, you'll find a great deal of structure, systems processes, and norms that appear to have been in existence since the beginning of time. "We've always done it that way" can be heard echoing through the halls of organizations where paintings of legacy leaders line the walls.

The talent that's best suited for this type of organization are yes people. This species of employee goes with the flow without question. They like structure, and they find comfort in operating in a world where things remain consistent and predictable.

Innovation

A culture of innovation is a culture in which conventional ideas fall by the wayside—or are thrown out the window. This type of culture is commonly found in start-ups, high-growth organizations, and groundbreaking companies. These companies push themselves to stay on the cutting edge of industry trends and developments. Strict lines of communication and structural hierarchies often give way for the sake of airing out innovative ideas and working through untested solutions. Companies in this space are breeding grounds for fertile new concepts.

People who thrive in innovative work environments are the pioneers who embrace change. These employees are not afraid to challenge the status quo, and they are constantly scanning for ways to improve systems, products, and the delivery of services. This species of talent has a high level of stamina; it is *not* risk averse, and it is extremely creative.

Empowerment

Empowerment cultures are those in which all employees feel valued. Regardless of position, rank, or length of service, employees are meant to feel as if their role in the business is critical for operational success. Employees at all levels of the organization are comfortable approaching their superiors with questions and suggestions. Should a conflict arise, steps are taken to make employees feel as if they stand on equal footing with one another. Bona fide requests for bonuses, wage increases, and position changes are seriously considered and are granted when appropriate.

Individuals who are confident and comfortable standing their ground are ideal hires for these types of organizations. People with low self-esteem need not apply! Those who enjoy working in an environment where promotions and pay raises are awarded based on contribution—not time spent in the job—will be a great fit for this type of climate.

Class System

Professional services firms are the first thing that come to mind when I think about the class system of culture. Hiring decisions and promotions are made based on lineage. If employees are born into the right family and attended the right schools, they are quickly ushered in. These employees are then groomed to move up in the organization. Everyone else is pretty much a second-class citizen.

Talent from top-flight schools like Harvard, Yale, and Princeton generally do well in these types of work environments, as these people are accustomed to being among the elite. When staffing this kind of organization, look for high achievers who understand the inner workings of distinctly competitive environments.

Family Business

Family businesses are notorious for nepotism, which is fine if your last name matches that of the person whose name is on the front door. The family business culture is also highly political, as family members battle it out to secure their legacy.

Adjusting to this type of environment can be challenging for some. When possible, look for candidates who have experience working in family businesses. Candidates who are accustomed to working in a matrix organization may be a good fit as well; it's not uncommon to have more than one boss in a family-owned business. Look for employees who have realistic expectations in terms of career advancement, as opportunities in these climates can be limited.

Where to Dig for Talent

If you've ever been to an amusement park, you'll know exactly what I mean when I tell you to "go left" when searching for talent. If you step back and watch all the people flooding into the park the moment the gates open, you'll notice an interesting phenomenon. The majority of people will go through the turnstiles and turn to the right. To the right, amusement-goers will find big crowds of people, long lines, and lots of frustrated visitors. Meanwhile, people who enter and head left have significantly shorter wait times for rides, food, and the purchase of park souvenirs. A comparable thing happens in the hunt for talent. Employers unthinkingly follow the crowd, when they should be scouring for talent in places that competitors frequently overlook.

You can unearth a gold mine of talent when you dig where no one else is digging.

Go for a Ride

I'm always amazed by how many people who use ride-sharing services like Lyft and Uber ride in silence. I always engage my driver in conversation and have discovered an incredible pool of talent that's yours for the asking. Many drivers are earning money on the side while working toward college degrees. Others already have degrees and are between jobs. A number of drivers are former professionals who have turned to driving because their employers were unable to offer them the flexibility they needed to balance the demands of work and family. The list goes on and on.

Not one of these people grew up dreaming of driving for a living, but here they are. The next time you slip into the back seat of one of these cars, put your phone down and start a conversation with your driver. This person may be the perfect candidate for the job you are trying to fill.

Try the Starbucks Strategy

Every day, millions of people across the world line up at places like Starbucks for their morning lattes, with only caffeine on their minds. Most people don't give any consideration to the individuals making their drinks, nor do they acknowledge the people taking their orders. Some people order their coffee through the store's on-line app and have minimal personal interactions with their baristas. If this sounds like you, then you are missing out on a huge opportunity to secure talent.

In April of 2015, Starbucks began offering their employees full tuition at Arizona State University's online program. This initiative affords both full-time and part-time employees without a four-year degree the opportunity to earn a bachelor's degree for free. Employees have no obligation to remain at Starbucks after they graduate. And as I write this, Disney announced that they will pay full tuition, books, and materials, for hourly workers who want to earn a degree—including a master's degree! So, what does this mean for you?

The person serving you in a coffee shop or greeting you at a Disney park might be working at one of these places to better themselves. And who wouldn't want to hire someone who is willing to do whatever it takes to grow? Keep this in mind the next time you are waited on by someone who could very well be a perfect addition to your team.

Look for Those Who Are Fifty, Full of Energy, and Fired Up for Work

Is it me or are employees at companies getting younger? Some-where along the line, people reach an age where they are no longer viewed as valuable contributors by employers. In some organizations, this may happen when you hit age forty, and in others, fifty seems to be the magic number. This trend is happening across all industries. Today, companies are falling over one another to snag their share of younger workers. Just because everyone is doing this doesn't mean you should as well. Go against the grain. Seek out the experienced workers that others are ignoring.

There are many benefits to hiring mature workers, including the fact that most won't be dragging themselves into work after a late night of partying, nor will they be demanding corner offices (or any office for that matter) after their first week of employment. Older workers have considerably more experience than their younger counterparts, which means you won't need to invest a ton of money bringing them up to speed. The best part is, because other companies are focusing on younger workers, you are less likely to get into a bidding war to secure this level of talent.

Give Non-degreed Applicants a Chance

Would you pass on hiring Facebook CEO Mark Zuckerberg simply because he doesn't have a college degree? How about Richard Branson, CEO of Virgin Group—or Bill Gates, former CEO of Microsoft? I doubt it. Yet some 61 percent of employers have rejected applicants with the requisite skills and experience, according to a 2017 study conducted by Harvard Business School.[1] The reason? The HBS study reports that these rejections were a result of only one factor: the simple fact that the applicants in question did not have a college degree. If current trends continue, the authors explain that "as many as 6.2 million workers could be affected by degree inflation—meaning their lack of a bachelor's degree could preclude them from qualifying for the same job with another employer."

For example, in 2015, 67 percent of production supervisor job postings asked for a college degree, but only 16 percent of employed production supervisors had one. According to analyses, the authors of the 2017 Harvard Business School study conclude that more than six million jobs are currently at risk of degree inflation. When you insist that workers have college degrees, your labor costs are artificially inflated; at the same time, the labor pool available to you is significantly decreased.

Think about the results you want people to achieve, and then sort out whether a degree is a "must have" or simply a "nice to have." If you can widen your net ever so slightly, you'll have way more candidates to choose from. And if a degree is critical for success in your organization, you can follow the lead of companies like Starbucks and Disney and offer to reimburse the cost of tuition for those candidates who agree to return to school in the evenings to complete their education.

Budding Talent

I bet there are a bunch of people in your own organization who are about to blossom. Then why do so many companies look to the outside when filling jobs, when talent is right under their noses?

This phenomenon happens for a number of reasons, including outdated personnel policies and office politics. Let's start with outdated policies. Many companies have policies stating that an employee must be in his or her job for at least six months before being eligible for a promotion or a transfer. This policy may have been appropriate when employers had the upper hand in terms of hiring. However, this rule makes no sense today, given how easily employees can find jobs that are a step up from the one they already have.

If you've got an employee who is ready to advance or to try something new, then let them—or someone else will! In fact, yesterday I was talking with a CEO about this. We were discussing how tight the labor market is for entry-level café workers. He's identified several companies that are making aggressive attempts to poach his workers. He's being proactive in his attempts to ward them off. Managers are now required to have conversations every thirty days with their employees regarding performance and future opportunities with the company. When necessary, they accelerate the promotion schedule they typically follow. Workers are encouraged to follow their passions. Employees can try out jobs in other departments before committing to a new career path. They can also return to their original roles, should they decide they were happier where they were.

Office politics is a known killer of budding talent. This occurs when leaders put themselves before their people. For example, a leader discourages an employee from considering an opportunity elsewhere in the organization because she doesn't want to lose an employee who makes her look good. Or a manager does nothing to help his employee land a new position in another department because he feels threatened by that leader.

Remember: If you don't help your people grow, they'll pull up stakes and go elsewhere.

Military Veterans and Active Military Spouses

According to the Department of Labor, the veteran unemployment rate for military vets as of July 2018, was 3.0 percent.[2] So why am I telling you to seek out what appears to be this scarce source of talent? Because the numbers don't paint the full picture. Veterans who have given up on finding a job altogether, and those who are underemployed, are not reported in these numbers.

Nearly a third of veterans are underemployed, according to a study from ZipRecruiter and Call of Duty Endowment,[3] a nonprofit foundation that helps veterans find jobs. This means they are working a job that they are overqualified for, which is where you come in.

These men and women have sacrificed a lot to serve our nation. Thank them for their service by seeking them out and offering job opportunities that are in line with their skill level. Statistics show that veteran turnover is lower throughout the arc of a veteran's career than turnover of nonveterans. Additionally, a majority of employers report that veterans perform "better than" or "much better than" non-veterans. Now can you see why I'm calling attention to this hidden patch of talent?

There are a number of government and state agencies that can connect you to veterans. You can also have job postings on your company website automatically included on The National Exchange, a daily government feed delivered directly to veterans, at no cost to you.

And let's not forget about the men and women who make it possible for many active military personnel to serve. Active military spouses are often overlooked by employers who fear it's only a matter of time before they are forced to relocate. Their loss is your gain. Today, many jobs can be done remotely. Before you go the more traditional route of posting jobs on the big name boards, check out the Military Spouse Employment Partnership. This is a site created by the Department of Defense to connect employers and military spouses. There are a lot less companies posting here than on more traditional boards, which means you stand a better chance to secure talent.

How Leaders Can Create and Sustain Flourishing Subcultures

As I've mentioned earlier, it's important to remember that organizations have subcultures. This is why it's not uncommon to hear one person say that a particular organization has a great company culture, while someone else is telling a friend how terrible it is to work for the very same company. Subcultures vary, depending on who is in charge of a particular department or the workgroup. Remember this when promoting or hiring people into leadership roles.

A leader's values and beliefs greatly influence the employee experience—perhaps even more so than the overall culture in the organization. If you don't like what people are saying to others about working in your department, then change the narrative. Of course, to do so, you have to change your own behavior first.

Executive Coaching

You don't have to be the CEO of your organization to benefit from executive coaching (although CEOs can certainly benefit from it). If you are a middle manager, you are probably responsible for overseeing a subset of the daily operations that support the organization's mission. *You* may think you're doing a stellar job leading your team. However, perception is what matters most. An executive coach can help you see what you may be missing. Most executive coaches will do a 360-degree assessment, which is designed to give you a panoramic view of your leadership capabilities. The coach surveys or interviews your team members, boss, and peers regarding your leadership style. When conducting interviews, it's not uncommon for a coach to uncover other issues impacting the broader corporate culture as well.

Having this information can be quite beneficial for a leader looking to improve team, department, or company-wide culture. First, you will gain a transparent analysis of exactly what behaviors you need to work on to become a more effective leader. In turn, this will have a direct impact on how team members feel about their particular work environment. You also get the side benefit of discovering issues that could be negatively affecting how people feel about their larger departments, or about the organization as a whole. This is information that your coach can help you leverage to improve your company, while further securing your place within it.

Some of these issues may be fairly easy to address. For example, you might discover that employees are frustrated with your lack of flexibility in terms of their work schedules. A good coach can provide guidance and help a leader become more employee focused. In this scenario, your coach may recommend a quick fix such as a few adjustments on either side of the clock. This will help you demonstrate your commitment to improving the employee experience.

If you are in the C-suite, you're probably focusing on company strategy, revenue growth, profitability, and keeping your stock price up (if you're a publicly traded company). Blind spots are less obvious when things appear to be going well. But maybe, with some outside help, you could be doing even better. It is easy for executives to become almost strictly inward looking, especially when they have been very successful. But these blind spots can become devastating when performance moves in the other direction. A good, neutral assessment can provide clarity for executives.

Finally, it's important to remember that office politics exist in every organization. This makes the coaching environment a rare safe place to think through various topics. You may have ideas that you aren't ready to openly share with other executives, until you've had the opportunity to fully flesh them out. Maybe you have the next groundbreaking innovation for your company under your hat, and you just need someone to help you figure out the best way to present your new solution. Executive coaching provides a safe haven to have these conversations, and this is one of the top reasons that executives hire me to be their guide. I'm able to provide a perspective that those in the organization either can't, or won't— for fear their job may be on the line.

BYO Nutrients

An organization won't necessarily offer to provide you with executive coaching under the company budget. If you ask, and your request is denied, consider investing in yourself. Trust me, when employees are lining up outside your office door to work for you, you will see your investment paid back in hefty dividends. You may receive an unexpected promotion (along with a pay increase) or be assigned a plum project that could help you leap to the next level in your organization.

Selecting the right coach is a personal matter. However, if you are looking to shift the culture in your company or work area, look for someone with a track record of helping leaders create work environments where employees love to come to work, and customers love doing business.

Applying the Knowledge

The following questions will help you identify and nurture the right talent for your environment:

- ¤ What words would you use to describe the culture in your organization?

- ¤ Given your company culture, what characteristics should you be looking at when seeking and assessing talent?

- ¤ Which sources of hidden talent will you include in your evergreen talent strategy? (Feel free to add some that you've discovered on your own.)

- ¤ What personnel policies need to be eliminated or revised?

- ¤ How will you address those leaders who are preventing their people from considering new opportunities in your organization?

- ¤ Do you perceive different subcultures across your organization? From your position in the company, how can you positively influence the varying subcultures you observe?

- ¤ What steps will you take to improve the work experience for your people?

- ¤ What goals will you work toward if you have the resources to hire an executive coach? What specific outcomes would you like to see?

5.

Abundant Hiring: Sustainable Hiring Practices for Optimal Growth

I don't understand how leaders can entrust hiring, which is the most critical aspect of their job, to someone else. No one knows what you need more than you, nor can they ascertain fit like you can. It's time to stop delegating this duty to HR, and place responsibility for talent acquisition where it belongs—with the hiring manager.

The Leader's Role in Acquiring a Sustainable Workforce

I recently had a conversation with a department head at a major university. This leader shared with me how his organization's HR team was struggling to fill job openings in *their own* department. It was at this moment that the leader realized he could no longer sit back and wait for HR to deliver the talent needed to successfully run his department. He had to take matters into his own hands, which is exactly what you should be doing. The following are some reasons why you should be doing the same.

You aren't beholden to anyone. How often have you sat back and watched while peers get the lion's share of the candidates? As a consultant, I hear this complaint a lot. Perhaps other hiring managers have a better relationship with people in HR, or they are more responsive than you. Or maybe the people trying to staff your jobs don't have a clear understanding of the requirements needed to be successful in these roles. That would make sense, as those in HR are not working in your department. At the end of the day, the reason may not matter. Regardless, you are right where you started—in dire need of talent.

You control the results. When you take responsibility for the hiring cycle, you are in complete control of the results. Candidates are more likely to call you back directly than they are to return a phone call to someone in HR. You won't waste time sending emails back and forth to HR to coordinate schedules. Nor will you have to explain, for the fifth time, the skills needed to fill tech positions. You'll also be able to accelerate the hiring process, since you'll be eliminating the need for HR to screen candidates. And in today's tight labor market, anything you can do to speed up your interview process will give you a *huge* advantage over your competitors.

You know where you stand in terms of hiring. How often have you asked your HR partner where things are in terms of hiring and the response you receive is that they're working on it? Yep. I used to give that response a lot when I worked in HR.

In retrospect, there were times when I should have asked for help. For technical jobs, I'd screen resumes based on buzzwords—rather than on potential. I did this because, frankly, I had no idea what was really required to succeed in a technical role. I'm certain that I'm not the only HR worker who's been too embarrassed to speak up about this. Or I'd focus on filling jobs that were easier to staff. Why did I do this? Because I knew that my performance was being evaluated on the number of positions filled, rather than on my success in filling difficult jobs. Where is the incentive for HR to tackle hiring for your organization's more challenging roles?

I suspect that not a lot has changed since my days in HR, which is why you need to know at all times where things really stand in terms of hiring. The only way to do this is to be in full control of your own hiring.

How to Convince HR to Give You Control

I talked about how to overcome resistance to change in Chapter 3. As you look to take control of your own hiring process, you may want to reread this chapter. These nuggets of wisdom will help you immensely in the task ahead, which will be a dramatic shift for many.

HR departments have far more responsibilities these days than most can handle. Your offer of taking a huge task off of their plates will be well received—as long as you approach it in the right way. Storming into your HR department is never a good idea. And telling these employees that you're taking your job requisitions back because they've failed to staff your openings in a timely manner will result in a full-on turf war. HR will spout out statistics regarding all the great people they've sent your way, and they will go on to say how nonresponsive you or a member of your team has been in terms of candidate feedback. You'll reply by telling them how disappointed you are in the candidates submitted or the lack of applicants—and you may say other things you will live to regret.

Instead, position this move with HR's best interests in mind. Explain that you understand how difficult the hiring environment is, and how overwhelming this must be—given the plethora of other responsibilities delegated to HR. Let your HR partner know that you're going to use some of your own resources to fill job openings in your area. Ask rhetorical permission to come back to them, as you may want them to weigh in on a candidate that you are considering. Make your offer so compelling that few would say no.

Suppose you go to HR and receive pushback about company procedures. Don't despair. Take your plea to your boss, and ask for suggestions on how to change protocol or work around this situation. Most managers will gladly offer advice, as they are as concerned about the staffing of your department as you are. Remind your boss that reducing the time it takes from the first point of contact to job offer is critical these days, and that it can make a big difference in terms of whether your offer will be accepted or rejected by those top-choice candidates.

Flourishing in Your New Role as Evergreen Talent Curator

I'm not going to lie to you. At first, it may feel like you just made the biggest mistake of your life when taking full responsibility for curating your own talent. However, as you begin to see results (and you will), you'll wonder why you didn't do this sooner! Be realistic, and don't expect overnight success. However, be prepared for success! No doubt others will be asking you to share your talent-curating secrets, as soon as they see how successful you have become in this arena.

A Grassroots Approach to Evergreen Talent

Although many grassroots movements start from the ground up, in this case, I'm suggesting a hybrid model. In this model, CEOs work in tandem with leaders on the front lines to effect change. In my work with clients, I have found that the most successful change initiatives transpire when CEOs lead the charge in engaging people to move toward a shared vision. CEOs who involve others while providing support, both in terms of time and resources, will excel in this transformative mission. Those who go it alone, or who choose to push change down throughout the organization, may be left scratching their heads about why this didn't work.

For change to become part of the fabric of an organization, consider the following. According to global management firm McKinsey, "One of the biggest challenges to overcome, in terms of change, is the widely held management view that 'All we have to do is tell employees what we want, provide some training and rewards, and change will happen.'"[1] This approach may work when the desired results lie well within the existing capabilities of an organization—for instance, in the task of developing a product extension. But this basic formula falls far short when the change requires fundamentally new ways of doing business—like moving from a product orientation to a customer orientation. In these cases, embedded skills, systems, and attitudes are often immensely at odds with the new requirements. This means that a much more intensive process is needed to retool the organization to effect lasting change.

Evergreen talent is fundamentally a new way of doing business for most organizations, which means you'll need to approach this differently than other initiatives to create long-lasting change. Here's how to begin.

Shared Vision

Grassroots activism is about marshaling a group of people who are passionate about a cause, and mobilizing the power of their collective conviction to push for a different outcome. This kind of undertaking relies on individuals who are willing to drive the change they want to see from the ground up.

For this to happen, you need a shared vision that people can get behind. When people have a common vision, they share the same picture of success, which creates tremendous energy. To establish a shared vision, follow these three steps:

1. First, provide the destination. Let people know exactly where you are going.

2. Next, explain the "why" behind the vision. Why is this vision so important? How will the organization *and* the individuals be better off as a result of this new direction?

3. Then explain the "how." (Note: Gather feedback from those on the frontlines, in terms of what will work and what won't. This will help ensure that your "how" will actually produce the results you are seeking. Seeking out the feedback of frontline employees will also help to build buy-in from those responsible for implementing the vision.)

Let me share with you an example of an evergreen talent vision statement that I developed with one of my clients:

> *To build a workplace where employees love to come to work and customers love to do business, by attracting, developing, retaining, and engaging an inclusive, high-performing workforce.*

What if your organization's vision statement is set in stone—but it doesn't seem to relate to your team or department? You don't have to be a C-level executive to apply an inspiring mission. If you are a middle manager, think about ways that you can make your company's vision more relatable to the employees who work beneath you. You don't have to change the words, but you can offer to be the translator. Help your employees understand how their work ties into the greater mission and vision of the organization. You can even go so far as to create a vision statement specifically for your department.

Now, create your own. If you'd like to send your vision statement to me for feedback, you can do so by emailing me at *Roberta@MatusonConsulting.com.*

Tell a Story

It's common to start an issue-based campaign by talking about the goal, which may explain why so many great ideas never take flight. For people to embrace ideas, they need an emotional connection. One of the most effective ways to create an emotional connection is through storytelling. You want to create an image and inspire a feeling that allows others to say, "Hey, I can see myself as part of this." Let me share an example from my story bank.

Throughout my friend Ray Pawlicki's career as a CIO, he's paid a grand total of just *three* recruitment fees. *Ever*. This success didn't happen overnight. Pawlicki regularly spoke at conferences as well as roundtables, and he talked about what it was like to work at his company. He *committed* 15 percent to 20 percent of his time to create, understand, and nurture the culture of his company, and getting the word out there about his organization. Pawlicki explained to me that doing so can be a real competitive advantage, especially when trying to fill positions in finance, IT, research, and engineering—where good people are consistently hard to find. Pawlicki's reputation as a guy who really cares about his people made it much easier to compete for and win talent, especially when he was up against CIOs who either had a poor reputation—or no reputation at all. People never hesitated to refer candidates to Pawlicki, which helped him avoid paying the hefty recruitment fees that others were forced to pay when hiring IT staff.

If you're thinking maybe you'll try and poach Pawlicki from his current employer—as he's obviously got this system down—you'll want to think again. Last I heard, he's happily retired and serving on boards.

Pawlicki's track record is impressive when you consider how challenging it has always been to hire IT people. Whenever I share the story of how this CIO took control of his talent pipeline and developed his people, other technical leaders begin to see what's possible. It's not uncommon for them to rally and challenge themselves to beat this CIO's record!

Acknowledge Your Supporters

A grassroots movement is about building something that's sustainable. A great way to accomplish this is to acknowledge and promote the achievements of your most committed and successful supporters. Those who take control of their talent pipelines should be recognized and rewarded. You can do this by inviting participants to share their approaches to filling their pipelines at in-house company meetings. You can also highlight success stories in your employee newsletter and on your company intranet, and ask supporters to present at company off-sites or at industry association meetings.

Success breeds success, which means the more people hear about achievements, the more likely those people are to join in. It's also beneficial to learn from the mistakes of others. Encourage supporters to share disappointments they may have experienced in addition to successes to help others avoid similar pitfalls.

Kicking Your Movement into Hyper-Growth Mode

Cultivating a passionate group of "talent evangelists" is the best way to scale. These are people seeded throughout the organization who carry your message with them wherever they go.

To build momentum, you'll want to bring *all* employees into the fold. Encourage team members to get "social." Have them leverage their personal Instagram, LinkedIn, and Facebook accounts to get the word out about your organization's talent movement.

Meanwhile, you should be doing the same with your company social media accounts. Don't have these accounts yet? It's time to get with the times! If your organization is large, there should be someone equipped to handle getting these accounts humming on all cylinders. Not a large company with a dedicated marketing team or any time to spare? Hire a college student to work with you on social media, or consider offering a teenage son or daughter a modest stipend to get your media accounts up and running (and to help maintain them). And while you're at it, don't discount the power of video. All you need is one YouTube video to go viral, and your crusade will enter warp speed.

Recognize talent evangelists for their results. This can be done with promotions, the payment of bonuses, and opportunities to increase the visibility of these employees within the organization. When others see colleagues being recognized and rewarded, they'll be inspired to join your evergreen talent movement.

Five Ideas for Rapidly Sourcing and Hiring Talent

Okay, your team understands the many benefits associated with taking control of their hiring needs, and they're willing to give it a go. Your next move is to help team members score some wins. These initial slam dunks are important so your people remain on board and want to shout from the rooftops about how empowering it is to hire your own talent. Let's look at some ways to help them get started.

Employee Referrals

Lots of companies have employee referral programs, where workers receive compensation or gifts in return for referring a candidate who is hired. This is a terrific idea, as few workers are willing to risk their own reputation by introducing someone into the organization who they wouldn't be proud to work with. And who couldn't benefit from receiving extra money in their paycheck every now and again!

However, there is a common problem with these programs. They are poorly marketed, which means employees forget they exist the moment the hoopla ends. Don't believe me? Ask a few of your managers to describe your company's employee referral program. Don't be surprised if most are unable to answer this question.

Employee referral programs, or significant change to current programs, are usually introduced with a huge splash. Announcements are made at the all-hands company meeting, reminders are inserted into paycheck envelopes, and of course there's the occasional mention in the company employee newsletter. Then silence. Let's make sure this doesn't happen to you. Consider the following:

Educate your hiring managers. Share data and statistics with your executive team, directors, and hiring managers. Educate these stakeholders on companies who have reduced their time-to-fill and cost-per-hire metrics as a result of their employee referral program. In her article "5 Powerful Methods to Promote Your Employee Referral Program," author Kelly Martin shares some eye-opening stats from Hiring Insights that are worth relating to your people:

- 88 percent of employers rate employee referrals above all other sources for quality hires.
- 70 percent of referred employees have not changed positions since being hired.
- Two-thirds of referred employees have referred at least one person for a job at their company.

These statistics demonstrate that managers will have less work to do in backfilling their positions if they staff these openings with employee-referred candidates. It's also worth noting that employee referrals have excellent conversion rates from interview to hire, thereby saving the hiring manager the loss of time that occurs when candidates turn down offers.

Communicate in a memorable way. You need to promote your program on an ongoing basis in a memorable way. Seek the advice of the creative minds in your marketing department for ways to keep your messaging fresh.

Provide regular updates about new job opportunities to increase awareness and participation. And don't forget to share employee referral success stories to increase employee interest.

Encourage employees to socialize. Urge employees to get out of the office and attend industry events and community gatherings. Provide them with tips on how to network in person and online. Provide your employees with business cards they're proud to hand out. You never know when the next social engagement could lead to a stellar new hire.

Social Media

According to *The Recruiter Nation 2015 Study* by Jobvite, social media has become an almost universally adopted hiring tool. In this study, 92 percent of surveyed recruiters were using some form of social media as part of their process, 87 percent of recruiters were using LinkedIn, 55 percent were using Facebook, and 47 percent were using Twitter.[2] Recruiters were using new networks as well, with 3 percent using Snapchat during their process. This means that you can no longer afford to be antisocial.

One of the major advantages of social media is that recruiters and hiring managers are able to bypass gatekeepers. Savvy recruiters are taking this one step further and are using third-party LinkedIn browser extensions like Dux-Soup and LinMailPro to expand their networks exponentially, with minimal effort. (Note: Learn how to use these programs appropriately to ensure your LinkedIn account doesn't get placed on hold.) For example, LinMailPro allows you to personalize *and* automate private messages to your LinkedIn connections. Be sure your hiring team is fully trained on how to use the various social media outlets and extensions, and encourage them to try new platforms as they come online.

Evergreen Networking

Networking has always been in fashion, although lately it seems like networking is done via social media networks more than in person. This gives you a great opportunity to stand out in a space that is no longer overcrowded.

Make it a point to attend industry conferences and get to know the up-and-coming players. Consider speaking at your local Chamber of Commerce or at association meetings to build your visibility. Do this enough times, and people will start coming to you for advice on matters related to their careers. You'll then have a chance to suggest that they consider your organization for their next move.

When networking, it's always best to give before you ask. Let's look at how you can do this. Say yes to a request for an introduction to someone in your network. Agree to an informational interview for someone's family member or friend. Offer to be a resource for a colleague's child who is considering attending the college you graduated from. All of these things will increase your net worth in terms of networking.

Become an Employer of Choice

Being an employer of choice means an organization is considered a great place to work. And in this day and age, when job candidates have a ton of choices, who wouldn't want to be in this category? The employer of choice field might seem overcrowded these days, with just about every local publisher dishing out their own versions of the Best Places to Work awards.

The truth is, you can become an employer of choice without having to hire a full-time staff to promote your company during award season. And when you're able to do this, you'll find it much easier to fill jobs. Here are some ideas to get you started.

Dare to be different. Companies are pumping money into workplace perks like free beer, cool office slides, state-of-the-art fitness centers, and make-your-own sundae bars. Let me tell you something: All the free beer in the world won't make employees delusional enough to remain with a lousy boss!

What if you took some of the money being spent on over-the-top perks, and used it to develop great leaders? Sounds crazy, right?! Not really, especially when you consider that most employees don't leave their companies—they leave their managers. And when your employees leave, they don't hesitate to go onto Glassdoor and other sites where they can freely dish about their current and past employers, and tell others what their experience was like working for your company.

Attraction is in the eye of the beholder. This is why I recommend that you determine exactly who you are looking to attract before investing money in Ping Pong tables or an on-site tattoo parlor. For example, suppose you're looking to attract a highly educated workforce. This means there's a good chance the people you're looking to hire will have college debt. What do you think will impress them more, a company-sponsored program to help them reduce their student loan debt, or a lunchroom fridge fully stocked with free soda? Unsure of what your target employee values? Ask your current employees what factors most influenced their decision to accept a position with your company and what benefits they value most. Then ask them, what is the number-one benefit they *wish* they had? This information will tell you exactly what direction to go in to secure your target workforce through offering meaningful benefits.

Create an Employer Brand That Stands Tall

There are a lot of great companies out there, and yours may be one of them. However, this won't matter if you're a best-kept secret. The Internet has made it a lot easier to brand your organization as an employer of choice. It has also made it more difficult for those companies who lag behind the times because they stick out like a condemned house in a nice neighborhood. Look at your website as if you were selling your house. You only get one chance to make a first impression. It's doubtful that you'll be able to get people to return to your website if at first glance they don't like what they see. That's why you want to get your employer brand right—on your first attempt.

When working on branding, it's important to paint those you are trying to attract into the frame, so they can envision themselves working in your organization. When it comes to employer branding, looks certainly do matter.

The following is a case study that demonstrates how an employer brand can help or hurt efforts to attract talent.

I recently worked with a client who was struggling to bring in younger financial advisors to service his company's growing clientele of young professional workers. He came to me because he was having a difficult time attracting this demographic of worker to his firm. One look at the website and I instantly knew why. The website contained pictures of the senior leaders of the company, who all happened to be middle-aged white men. It's interesting to note that the photos did not accurately reflect the makeup of his firm as their workforce is, in fact, diverse. Yet, no one would have known this from looking at their company branding. At my suggestion, my client brought in a professional photographer to take photos of his employees in action. These images were much more vibrant than the ones of "four old men sitting around chatting" (his words, not mine). We reworked the content on the career page, and instead of focusing on what we hoped employees would do for the company, we talked about how the company serves their clients *and* their employees.

Within two months, my client had attracted and hired the perfect candidate. When asked why this candidate decided to join the firm, he said he visited the company's website and liked what he saw. Trust me, this never would have happened if my client hadn't focused on creating a more appealing employer brand.

Look at your website with an eye toward improving how prospective employees relate to your employer value proposition. Better yet, ask a friend to view your website and recruitment materials. Is your message so compelling that they were tempted to apply for a job? If not, why?

Applying the Knowledge

As you think about creating sustainable hiring practices for optimal growth, consider the following.

- ¤ How willing are you to take back responsibility for hiring?
- ¤ What steps will you take to make this happen?
- ¤ Prepare for your conversation with HR by creating a script you can use to take control of the hiring process.
- ¤ Create a plan to establish a grassroots evergreen talent movement.
- ¤ What ideas will you put into action to rapidly source and hire talent?
- ¤ What are two or three things you can immediately do to spark interest in your employee referral program?
- ¤ On a scale of 1–10 (with 10 being high), how would you rate your employer brand? If you rated your brand less than a 10, what steps can you take to get to a 10?

6.

Corporate Regeneration: Reinvigorating Dormant Workers

It happens, even in the best of companies. Employees who were once highly engaged have become disenchanted. Upon reflection, you can often pinpoint the exact time and reason that an employee has gone dormant. It is valuable to examine these factors, to prevent other engaged employees from withering in place.

The Real Truth About Employee Engagement

Many organizations struggle with employee "engagement," an employee's willingness to go above and beyond the call of duty. That's because companies are focusing on the wrong things. Employee engagement is not a program—it's an outcome. Nevertheless, companies spend billions of dollars on employee engagement programs, with the hope that something will stick. Don't make the same mistake.

Let's look at why employees wither on the vine, and what you can do to prevent this.

One-size-fits-all approach to management. A one-size-fits-all approach to management fits exactly no one. According to Quantum Workplace's 2018 Employee Engagement Trends Report, newer employees want opportunities, and tenured employees want to feel valued.[1]

When examining the engagement drivers of differently tenured employees, two insights were revealed: The longer employees work at an organization, the more these employees need to feel valued by their leaders. Newer employees, on the other hand, are more driven by professional growth and career development opportunities.

To keep employees engaged, encourage leaders to flex their management style when working with team members. Remind them that equal is not fair. If you treat your superstars the same way you treat your mediocre employees, it won't be long before mediocrity becomes the new norm.

No room for growth. Think back to all the promises that were made to you when you first started a new job. How many of those assurances panned out? Many new hires (and seasoned veterans as well) are promised the sun, the moon, and promotions—only to discover they've been sold a bill of goods. Others find themselves in situations they hadn't anticipated. For example, an employee may be assigned a new boss who doesn't feel the need to honor a commitment made by someone else. Or perhaps there is a downturn in business, resulting in fewer opportunities for everyone.

Here's the thing about growth. There are many ways for employees to experience growth at work. Leaders can appoint employees to a company task force, where they'll be exposed to new ideas while gaining valuable expertise. Supervisors can ask highly valued employees to mentor others in the organization. Managers can offer employees the opportunity to rotate in and out of other departments, where employees will inevitably pick up new skills and identify new strengths they never even knew they had. Which brings me to my third point.

Lack of employee development. According to LinkedIn's 2018 Workforce Learning Report, a whopping 93 percent of employees would stay at a company longer if the company invested in their careers.[2] Development is no longer an optional perk or reserved for only certain positions. It's *expected* by today's talent. Development opportunities signal that an employer values their people and is actively interested in their employees' success—not just on the job, but over the long haul.

If you're not investing in your people, they'll turn their attention elsewhere and find someone who will. It's never been easier to develop employees, and it's certainly never been more affordable. Options for learning and development include free massive open online courses (MOOCs), subscription online learning options such as LinkedIn Learning, reimbursement for attendance at industry conferences and local association meetings, private or group coaching, and tuition reimbursement.

Poor leadership. I probably should have listed this first, as employees don't work for companies. They work for people. When I first started working for an overnight delivery service, I was highly engaged. I enjoyed the work; the company culture was a good fit, and I had no intentions of leaving anytime soon. That is, until my manager made some leadership decisions that demonstrated that my presence was no longer valued.

In retrospect, my boss probably never should have been a manager. This happens a lot. Many organizations aren't selective enough about whom they let into management. If you're good at your job, boom, you're promoted. If a management job opens up, and you're the only one to express an interest, the job is yours! This should never be the trajectory that lands someone in leadership, yet oftentimes, it is.

As I've stated in Chapter 2, there are several very important factors you should consider before promoting someone into management. This can't be overstated enough! If you need a refresher, please revisit this content.

Keep in mind that leadership is a journey. The best leaders are always learning. Those organizations that develop and support leaders at every stage of their careers will reap the many benefits associated with having a highly engaged workforce.

Overcrowded Work Spaces

Whoever came up with the concept of completely open work spaces should be made to spend the rest of their life in one. In theory, the idea of breaking down walls and having people working side by side with peers and supervisors sounds like a really cool concept. That is, until you find yourself sandwiched between a coworker who talks too loudly and someone who eats tuna fish salad all day. It's no wonder you can't find a conference room to use when you want privacy. That's because people have staked these out so they can get some work done.

All you have to do is walk into any open office environment and count the number of people who are wearing earbuds. So much for enhanced communication! When an employee can't get her job done because of all the distractions, it's not uncommon for that employee to work overtime to hit her deadlines. And if you're a professional who doesn't get paid for overtime, it doesn't take long for the frustration to kick in.

I get that you may not have the power to change the office layout. However, you are not completely powerless. You can honor an employee's request to work from home several days a week. By doing so, you may help to alleviate some of the stress an employee may be feeling. At the same time, you'll create some additional elbow room for those still working in the office.

Lack of purpose. When I first started working, there was no such thing as a search for purpose in the workplace. We were in the midst of a recession, and most of us were grateful to even have a job. What a difference a few decades makes (okay, maybe more than a few)!

Having a job is no longer the be-all and end-all for workers—especially younger workers. Today, people want to know that their work matters. They feel most satisfied when they know how their contribution makes a difference. To keep employees engaged, you'll need to remind them from time to time of the impact their work is having, both inside and outside of the organization. You can do this in a number of ways. Send an employee in person to deliver a product to one of your best customers. Take time to review customer testimonials or reviews as a team. Provide recognition for outstanding client feedback.

Empty promises. A fully engaged employee will quickly become a disengaged employee in the face of empty promises. This may include a commitment for a salary adjustment that somehow never comes to fruition, or an ever-elusive promotion. The list goes on and on.

The best way to prevent this from happening is to avoid making promises you may not be able to keep. Instead of saying, "You're doing an awesome job, Craig. No doubt the next promotion will go to you," consider tempering your enthusiasm. You might say instead: "You're doing a terrific job, Craig. Keep up the great work so that when our boss asks who's ready to be promoted, I can add your name to the list."

Lack of autonomy. Surveys consistently show that what employees want most is autonomy. I've said this before, and I'll say it again: Employees want control over the way their work gets done. Now if we could only convince all those micromanagers to let go. We can, and we must! Otherwise, those who remain in your employ will be nothing more than worker bees.

Micromanagement is about lack of trust. Micromanagers subscribe to the belief that if you want something done right, you must do it yourself. If supervisors continue to manage this way, their wishes will come true! They'll be able to do everything themselves when their team goes AWOL.

Help your leaders understand why letting go of control is in their best interests. For example, when leaders give their employees more autonomy, they simultaneously free up their own energy to work on higher level projects. This may eventually lead to a promotion for savvy supervisors. They'll be able to leave the office on time, and make it to their kids' school play. They won't have to work so hard filling open positions because others in the organization will want to join their teams. They'll have a more engaged workforce, which in turn will result in higher levels of productivity. Once leaders understand why it's in their best interests to give people autonomy, most will step back and allow team members to step up and do their jobs.

Employees outgrowing the organization. The number of US employees willing to go above and beyond the call of duty in the workplace has dropped by nearly 10 percentage points over the last three years, according to a new report from research and advisory firm Gartner.[3] What might be behind this decline? Lack of opportunities for career growth appears to be a likely answer. Nearly 40 percent of American workers surveyed by Gartner ranked lack of future career opportunities as the most dissatisfying attribute at a previous job.

Take a look at the way roles are structured in your company, with an eye toward adding levels within job families. For example, suppose your customer service department consists of two positions—customer service representative and manager. Consider adding new job titles that allow employees to promote in place once they've achieved certain levels of proficiency. In this example, a customer service representative could promote to a level II or level III position, and may even move into a lead customer service representative role. A change like this will provide employees with the career growth they desire. This will dramatically help to lower the number of employees who disengage when they feel that their careers are at a standstill.

How to Determine If Talent Is Worth Rejuvenating

Not everyone who is dying on the vine is worth revitalizing! The other day, I received a call from a client who was seeking advice about firing an employee who wasn't working out. I asked him when he decided he needed to do this. He said, "Twenty years ago!" Some of you may be smiling as you read this story, and no doubt there are a number of you saying, "Hmm . . . why is she writing about me?"

Ask yourself the following—*before* trying to save an employee who has gone dormant:

- ¤ If I had to do it over again, would I still hire this person?
- ¤ If I didn't have to deal with HR or legal, would I have cut this person from the team a long time ago?
- ¤ How likely is it that I can replace this person with a more productive employee?
- ¤ How much better would my life be if this person were no longer with the organization?
- ¤ Is this person preventing me from promoting a valuable employee because he is occupying a spot but no longer worthy of it?
- ¤ Would the organization as a whole be better off with or without this person?

- ⌗ How is this person's behavior impacting her direct reports and the rest of the team?

- ⌗ Will our customers be better served by someone else in this role?

- ⌗ What impact—if any—will keeping this employee have on my reputation within the organization?

- ⌗ Would this person be better off working elsewhere?

Your responses to these questions will determine where you go from here. If you believe this person is salvageable, you'll want to arrange whatever training or coaching is needed to get this person's performance to the level it needs to be. If it appears it's time to cut your losses, then you'll need to head straight to HR for advice on how to best transition this person out of the organization. Smaller companies without access to this type of support may wish to consult with a labor attorney to ensure that the situation is handled properly.

The TLC Approach to Reviving Talent

Let's suppose you've made the decision to try and bring your withered employee back into the fold. Perhaps you've realized that you failed to set this person up for success—or you discover that it's next to impossible to find a replacement. Regardless of the reason, you'll need a solid strategy to help your employee successfully re-engage. Try using my TLC (tend, lift, and champion) approach to reviving talent.

Tend. Lots of us have been in situations where if we're not the ones most in need of help, we are left to our own devices. Very little in the way of care and attention is bestowed on us. In fact, I can't even count the number of times when I asked myself, "If I didn't show up for work tomorrow, would my boss even notice?" This rings particularly true for remote workers, as they are very much out of sight—*and* often out of mind.

Once you commit to helping an employee reach her potential, then you need to make this employee your priority. Schedule time to meet weekly (or more frequently if needed), and note this on your calendar. Do your best to keep all appointments. Check in from time to time, and make yourself available should your team member need additional assistance. This employee will need as many nutrients as you can afford to give if you want her to blossom for another season.

Lift. Hopefully, you've had at least one conversation with your employee about how his performance is not up to standards and have discussed your expectations in terms of improvement. Conversations about negative performance can leave an already struggling employee feeling deflated and defeated. To turn a situation like this around, you'll need to help lift the spirit of your employee—so she can see that there is hope on the horizon.

Start by setting goals that are attainable. Be on the lookout for opportunities to catch your employee doing something right. This will help to reinforce positive behavior. Should she begin to head off in the wrong direction, gently guide her back on track. It's also helpful to remind your employee every now and again that you are glad she's a part of your team.

Champion. There are no secrets in organizations, which means that if you have an employee who is struggling, others know about this. When this occurs, people tend to keep their distance. And when this happens, the employee is no longer kept in the loop. It's hard to be effective in your job when you don't have access to information. As your employee's supervisor, this is where you come in.

You need to be out there championing on behalf of your people. Let your boss know of your plan to work more closely with this employee, and keep your boss informed of your employee's progress. Run interference if you observe situations where others may unknowingly, or intentionally, impact your employee's ability to succeed. Once your employee starts to excel again, look for opportunities to make this known to a wider audience within the organization.

What to Do When You Can't Bring Someone Back to Life

There will be times when no matter how hard you try, you will not be able to revive a disengaged employee. The truth is, you can't want more for an employee than they want for themselves. It's time to cut your losses. Read on, and I'll tell you how in the next chapter.

Applying the Knowledge

Think about the following as you look to reinvigorate dormant workers:

- ⌥ In your organization, is employee engagement a program or an outcome? If it's a program, what can you personally do to shift your mind-set to focus on outcomes?

- ⌥ What should you consider before promoting someone into a leadership role?

- ⌥ Make a list of anyone on your team who has gone dormant. Then schedule a meeting to create a plan that will help them blossom again.

- ⌥ Review the reasons why employees wither on the vine. Identify any areas where there is room for improvement; then, commit to doing things differently.

- ⌥ What questions will you ask yourself before trying to save a dormant employee?

- Identify employees in need of TLC.
- List employees who need to be transitioned out of the organization. Include the date by which this will be completed.

III

Cultivating Your Workforce

7.

The Need to Weed:
Making Room for New Growth
to Flourish

I can't tell you how many times my husband and I have stood in front of our garden, arguing over whether a thriving plant is a weed, or something we actually planted. Weeds often look like plantings to the untrained eye. The same is true in organizations. You've got employees passing as workers, although they are adding little in terms of value to the organization. I've identified four species of employees that need to be eradicated from your organization.

1. **The minimalist.** This breed of employee is one of the more common species found in organizations. These employees do what's required of them and nothing more. Leaders look at these workers and think, "I've had worse employees. At least they're doing their job."

2. **The silent complainer (his face says it all).** These are the employees who walk around with a disgruntled look on their faces. More than likely, you've encountered one or

more of these employees when dining out, shopping, or standing in line at your local Department of Motor Vehicles office. What you may not realize is that these people also reside in offices around the globe.

Leaders often overlook these workers because they usually don't cause a ruckus. Unfortunately, the same can't be said for customers and clients. Some will make a stink, and others will quietly take their business elsewhere.

3. **The passive-aggressive employee.** This species tells you what you want to hear, and then does what they want. It's easy for busy managers to overlook this group of employees. It usually takes some time before supervisors realize that these employees aren't actually following through on their commitments. Even when the problem is recognized, it's not uncommon for managers to simply complete their employees' tasks themselves.

4. **The inconsistent performer.** These employees have a track record of doing great work—that is, some of the time. Other times, their performance is a complete disaster. The problem for managers who oversee these workers is that they have no way to predict how a project will go. Therefore, managers spend countless hours closely monitoring the work of these employees to ensure they remain on track.

The Impact Nonperformers and Disengaged Employees Have on Evergreen Talent

Companies are filled with nonperformers who are permitted to stay. My guess is that there are nonperformers in your organization as well. Let's take a look at the impact underperforming employees have on organizations and business growth. Then, you can decide for yourself if the time has come for you to do some corporate pruning.

Nonperformers prevent up-and-coming talent from sprouting. I frequently hear stories from talented people who have left their organizations because there was no room for growth. Tales of "protected" managers are common. They tell me it would take an act of God to have these people removed. They look at their future and realize their boss will never leave, and therefore, there is no upward movement for them in the organization. They do what many frustrated employees do. They decide to look for a new opportunity elsewhere.

Weak leaders rarely hire people who are stronger than they are because that would only call attention to their deficiencies. Subpar managers replace employees who leave with other subpar people to ensure that their place in the organization remains safe.

I challenge you to think about how many talented people you've lost because they felt stifled. Even one is too many.

The creation of dismal growing conditions. I can personally attest to what it's like to work in an environment with a bunch of miserable people. I worked in one organization where there were enough of these people to start a whole separate company! Of course, no organization intentionally becomes a miserable place to work. This happens over time, when leaders fail to pluck out employees whose negativity contaminates the environment.

Dealing with toxic employees is imperative. If you fail to eradicate these people, they will poison the rest of the organization. You may not be able to weed them out all at once, but you have to start somewhere. Read on to see why it's so important to do this now, rather than later.

Tarnished employer brands. What's the first thing people do when they hear about a job opening? They'll seek out the opinion of a friend who is familiar with the company, or they'll go onto *Glassdoor.com* and scan the reviews written by current and former employees. It only takes a few negative comments like, "Run for the hills!" or "This is the worst place I've ever worked" to taint your company's reputation.

The people who write negative reviews are the ones who are dismayed. This is why it's critical to move employees who are visibly unhappy out of the organization promptly, unless you truly believe you can quickly bring them back into the fold.

Increase in unwanted employee turnover. When people tire of working with a team of disengaged employees, they will leave. Others will take notice and will soon follow suit. Before long, some of your best employees will be gone.

People have a choice today in terms of employers. Your job is to ensure that people *choose* to work for you. It's no secret that A-level players want to work with other A-level players. Take a look at your team and ask yourself: If I had the opportunity to do it again, would I make the same hiring decisions? If the answer is no, then you know what you need to do next.

Lower company earnings. Gallup is an organization that is known for their groundbreaking research in the area of employee engagement. The article "How Employee Engagement Drives Growth," found on the Gallup website and written by Susan Sorenson, highlights a Gallup finding that has been a game changer for many. Gallup has found that companies with highly engaged workforces have been shown to outperform their peers by 147 percent in earnings per share. It stands to reason that companies with disengaged workforces have lower earnings per share. Some disengaged employees will stop at nothing to destroy a work unit—or an entire business. Why take this risk?

Determining Which Employees to Keep

My clients often ask me what factors to consider when assessing which team members to keep and which should be plucked. I tell them to think about the following:

Employee contribution. How is the organization better off as a result of team members being there? In other words, what (if any) contribution is the employee making toward the achievement of departmental goals? Company goals? If the employee went away tomorrow, would anyone notice?

Potential. Organizations are constantly changing, which means that the job someone is doing today might look completely different a year from now. Does the employee have the potential to adapt? Can that person do more than what's required in their current role, or has he reached his limit?

Future needs. What does the future look like for your organization? Will you be entering global markets? Is the plan to shift from brick-and-mortar stores to online retail sales? Are there plans to expand through acquisitions? What are the future needs of the organization in terms of skills? Will there be a place in the next rendition of the company for team members? Can they retool, or have they reached the end of the road in your organization?

The cost of doing nothing. My favorite question to ask clients is this: What will happen if you do nothing? If you stick your head in the sand and do nothing, what will it cost you in terms of productivity, innovation, market share, etc.? The response I usually hear after clients have time to reflect is, "Wow! I never thought of it that way." I even had one client tell me he would leave the organization—and he was the owner!

Timeless Tips for Tactful Terminations

I think it's important to cover the topic of how to conduct an employee termination—while leaving this person's heart intact. It's surprising how many leaders are inept at this. It's time to learn how to let someone go in a way that will have them thanking you on the way out the door. Once you've got this mastered, you'll be more apt to prune—rather than waiting for the big corporate bulldozer to arrive and bail you out.

Here are some timeless tips to help you smoothly transition employees out of your organization.

Treat people with respect. You would think this would happen naturally. The reality is, it doesn't. Being terminated can be as stressful as the death of a loved one or a divorce. Recognize that this will be a very difficult moment for the employee on the chopping block, and do your best to be respectful. This means finding a room with privacy and giving the employee ample time to process what has just happened. Make sure she is ready before you send her back to her cubicle to pack up her belongings. If at all possible, avoid what I call the "perp walk." This is where security escorts the employee off the grounds while other employees anxiously watch from the sidelines. All this does is make the employee feel like a criminal, when their only crime might be poor job performance.

Avoid surprises. As noted in earlier chapters, strong leaders provide their people with continuous feedback. This means that an employee's termination should never come as a surprise. If you believe an employee may be caught off guard by termination, then it's time to retrace your steps. A more honest conversation regarding the situation may be warranted before you move to terminate this employee.

Be prepared. It's easy to get pulled off course when terminating an employee—especially if you've been asked to do this for reasons you don't completely support. Jot down some speaking points, and refer to them during the meeting. This will help you avoid saying something like, "You're one of my stronger players," followed by, "I have to let you go." A misstep like this could come back to haunt you, should the employee decide to sue.

Focus the conversation on job performance. Resist the temptation to tell the employee that they have a bad attitude. Without specific examples, this kind of explanation will mean nothing to them. Instead, focus your discussion on performance-related issues. Rather than telling an employee that you are firing him because his coworkers don't like him, cite specific examples of how this person's interactions have consistently negatively impacted his ability to achieve agreed-upon goals.

Be brief. This is neither the time nor the place to rehash all the events that have led up to the termination conversation. The less that is said, the better. No doubt the employee you are terminating would like to get out of your office as quickly as possible, and most likely you feel the same way. Be succinct and tell the employee why he or she is being let go. Give them a moment to process what is being said. Then proceed with the specifics, including the official termination date, extension of employee benefits (if appropriate), what the former employee's final paycheck consists of and when she will receive it, and instructions on how to file for unemployment (if appropriate).

Leave the door open. If an employee is being let go because the position is no longer needed, encourage him to apply again when there are new opportunities. Companies like Kronos Incorporated—which has been named to the *Boston Globe*'s annual Top Places to Work ranking and was the number-one best place to work in the Largest Company category for 2018—is great at this. Kronos has found that some of their best hires are people who have left the company and returned at a later date. In his book, *WorkInspired*, Kronos CEO Aron Ain writes about boomerang employees in great detail. In fact, sometimes Ain's company hires back boomerang employees just weeks after they've left! This would not be possible if managers did not treat exiting employees on the way out with compassion.

How to Organically Prevent Weeds from Sprouting

Let's assume you've looked closely at your team and made the necessary changes. If you continue to lead the way you've always managed, more weeds will undoubtedly sprout. You can organically prevent another infestation of undesirable employees from taking over your talent beds.

Start by keeping the lines of communication open. Believe it or not, most people don't wake up one day and decide to be your worst nightmare. Nor do most employees intentionally go from happy at work to downright miserable to be around. Check in frequently with your people. Carve out time weekly for what I refer to as "time out for a coffee." This is where you invite people into your office to have a cup of coffee or tea. No office? No problem. You can invite team members to join you in the lunchroom or at the local coffee shop. You'd be surprised how relaxed and open people are when they have a cup in hand! This is your opportunity to find out what's really on people's minds, and to offer support where needed. This approach will help you recenter employees who might be moving toward disengagement.

When communicating with employees, remember that transparency is vital. In my book *The Magnetic Leader* (Taylor and Francis, 2017), I list transparency as one of the seven attributes that define a magnetic leader. Leaders who are transparent are consistently honest and open in their communication with their employees. As a result, people never have to guess what these leaders really mean when they say something.

When you are transparent with people, they know exactly where they stand. This builds trust and, in turn, employee engagement. Think about this the next time you are tempted to sugarcoat a conversation with an employee regarding performance.

Another way to prevent employees from moving into the ranks of the disengaged is to directly address all roots of conflict. I get that, for many, conflict is uncomfortable. But it doesn't have to be this way.

A strong leader gives employees the tools needed to resolve conflict situations on their own, rather than continuously playing the role of referee. The following are some suggestions to help you transition from referee to coach:

- Encourage employees to work things out on their own. Provide them with guidance.

- Ask employees what they've done to work out a situation.

- Look for core causes when conflict is brought to your attention.

- Redirect the person making the complaint back to the individual he or she is having the conflict with. Offer suggestions on how to approach this person without being defensive.

- Request this person give you feedback on how things went. Offer additional feedback, if appropriate.

Since disagreement is inevitable, it makes good business sense to train employees and management on how to effectively deal with conflict in the workplace. In addition to direct training, employees will learn quickly when the leaders in your organization demonstrate the same straightforward approach to conflict resolution that they preach. Your investment will reap immediate dividends. Employees will spend less time focusing on one another and more time focusing on your customers.

Make it a point to speak with people when you first notice a problem. By doing so, you'll stand a much better chance of finding common ground before things get out of hand.

Tap into people's strengths. When you do, you'll notice that your employees will come alive. Studies consistently show that people who use their strengths report greater levels of well-being and increased progress toward their goals. Take the time to discover people's strengths, and find ways to incorporate those strengths each day. Development of employee strengths can include on-the-job opportunities, mentor coaching, and formal training. Keep in mind that it's not enough just to know people's strengths; employees need to be regularly doing what they're good at if you want to increase their likelihood of flourishing.

Applying the Knowledge

As you look to ensure there is room for new growth to flourish, consider the following:

- ♯ Start to recognize the four species (minimalist, silent complainer, passive-aggressive, inconsistent performer) of employees who need to be eradicated. Make a list of anyone on your team who falls into one or more of these categories. Next to their names, specify what you are committing to do to address the situation.

- ♯ What factors will you consider in determining whom to keep and whom to prune?

- ♯ Have you quickly and transparently addressed issues with withering employees? If not, what can you do to stop avoiding conflict and communicate as needed?

- ♯ Write down what might happen if you do nothing with employees who are disengaged. Look closely at the results to assess whether doing nothing is really your best option.

- ♯ How many talented people have you lost over the past year because they felt they had nowhere to go? Write down the names of these former employees, and commit to staying in touch. Reach out to them when an opportunity comes up, and see if they are willing to return.

¤ What three things will you commit to so you can organically prevent more disengaged employees from sprouting up?

¤ Write down the strengths of each of your direct reports. Make a note of several things you can do to help each person flourish.

8.

Growing Talent from Seedling to Redwood

Since the great recession of the late 2000s, we've been on one heck of a ride in terms of the US economy. The number of job openings in the United States hit a record high in 2019, with job openings exceeding the number of unemployed workers.

During the recession, few organizations gave much consideration to how employees felt about their employers. Companies weren't actively considering employee retention, nor were they doing much in terms of investing in the development of their people. Employers were in the driver's seat. Massive layoffs resulted in an abundance of available talent. Employers could easily hire experienced people who would stay, regardless of working conditions.

What a difference a few decades make! With the 2019 record high for job openings, employees have the upper hand—and employers know it. Companies are bending over backward to secure and retain talent.

It's estimated that job growth won't slow down anytime soon. Current demographics indicate that an influx of talent is not on the foreseeable horizon. And to make matters worse, a massive part of the American workforce is in the process of retiring. An article on the Motley Fool website titled "9 Baby-Boomer Statistics That Will Blow You Away," by Matthew Frankel, CFP, states that the AARP estimates that 10,000 Baby Boomers are reaching retirement age every day! So what does this mean for you?

It's time to toss out those five- or ten-year staffing plans because they are irrelevant. Furthermore, these plans give employers a false sense of security. I suggest that your horizon be no more than two years because things could change on a dime. Plan to review your talent strategy every six months, and make adjustments accordingly.

Instead of concentrating on long-term hiring strategies, you need to shift your focus to employee retention. In a zero-unemployment economy, talent poaching is what you need to be most concerned about. What are you doing to prevent theft of talent, and what changes will you make in your organization to make it easy to steal talent from others? To be successful in this endeavor, you'll need to have a clear understanding of what today's workers *really* want from their employers.

What Workers Want from Their Employers

Employees at various stages of their careers often have different wants and needs. However, across experience levels and professions, most employees would agree that the following concerns are at the top of their lists.

Great Leadership

It seems that every day there is a new article about another company providing crazy perks to employees. In their efforts to attract and retain workers, employers are trying to outdo each other with free snacks that are causing people to gain weight at work and personal assistants for every employee (okay, that perk *does* sound good to me!). At the end of the day, however, even a five-star chef dishing up lunch won't be enough to get your employees to remain with a boss or a company that has bad leadership.

In spite of billions of dollars being spent to improve the workplace, Gallup research suggests that 68 percent of employees are disengaged—meaning they don't really care what happens to the organization or to your customers.[1] This can be disastrous! Research has consistently shown that employees don't leave companies. They leave their bosses.

What if you took all this money you are spending on snacks, free lunches, beer, etc., and instead committed these resources to hiring and developing outstanding leaders? You'd still have a ton of money left over to invest in the development of *all* your team members!

Employee Development

There's a disconnect between what employees want and what employers believe they want, as evidenced in a poll conducted by Execu/Search.[2] When asked to rank a list of job characteristics in order of importance, most employers put salary and benefits at the top of the list. Given the same choices, however, 51 percent of employees and prospective hires gave "opportunity for professional development," including training and career planning, as their top priority. "Employees more than ever, especially millennials, want to be a part of a company they not only share common core values with but also help them grow as an individual both personally and professionally," states Alexis Davis, founder and CEO of H.K. Productions Inc. "Employee development is not simply a nicety; it is necessary for employee retention," says Davis. I couldn't agree more!

No one wants to go to work thinking, "Is this all there is?" Employees who reach this stage operate on automatic pilot and will eventually seek more challenging opportunities elsewhere. Later in this chapter, I'll offer up suggestions on how to provide development opportunities for all employees, regardless of budget.

Sense of Purpose

I graduated college during the great recession, when there was no such thing as a sense of purpose at work. You took whatever job you could find to pay your college loans or to feed your family. Things are completely different today. Employees of all generations are seeking workplaces that offer a sense of purpose. They want to know their work has meaning, and that they are helping to make the world a better place.

Leaders need to continually look for ways to help team members connect their work to the organization's sense of purpose, as this is something that is easily lost in the fast-paced world of business. Managers should articulate the vision, mission, strategy, and goals of the organization. Leaders need to demonstrate how these statements provide the context for individual employees' everyday contributions, explaining how these efforts help organizations achieve the greater whole. Individuals want to feel like they matter. Our current generation of workers needs to know that if they were to leave their job tomorrow, they'd be missed.

There are a number of ways leaders can help employees better understand the impact their work has on others. This includes welcoming employees from all levels of the organization to participate in establishing the organization's sense of purpose. This also includes inviting clients into the office so employees can hear directly from the people who are benefiting from their efforts. As a leader, you need to work to incorporate conversations about your organization's mission and purpose whenever the opportunity arises.

A word of caution: It is critical that the behavior of senior leadership is consistent with a company's stated purpose and values. Otherwise, these words will inevitably ring hollow. Employees will recognize insincerity and become cynical as a result. Conversely, authentic and consistent leadership behavior will demonstrate leaders' commitment to the stated purpose of their organization. This helps employees believe in the purpose themselves, and soon employees and leaders will be working together to achieve a common goal. Remember: Change is signaled from the top, and then it unfolds from the bottom.

Feedback

Why is it so difficult for leaders to give employees something they want and need, especially when it doesn't cost a dime? For me, that's the million-dollar question. I hope that reading this will inspire you to reconsider your approach to giving feedback.

During a performance review, I once had a boss tell me this: "You're not meeting my expectations, although I'm not sure I ever told you what they were." I sat there shocked. I then thought to myself, she went to Harvard, where they may have taught Mind Reading 101; I went to Northeastern University, where learning how to be a psychic was not part of the business curriculum. Seriously, people. How can your employees improve without direction and feedback?

I get that feedback can feel like conflict for some. And who can honestly say they love conflict? However, if you give people constructive feedback on an ongoing basis, you'll quickly see that it's not that difficult to do. Frame your feedback in a way that will help your employees improve and grow, and always be forthright with your people. I hope you'll give this a try. If you do, I'm confident that you'll soon appreciate the importance of delivering consistent, transparent, and actionable feedback.

Opportunity

Studies show that employees—especially Millennials—are interested in opportunities for growth. Believe it or not, employees actually factor this in when evaluating prospective employers! They also weight this heavily when considering their status with their current employer. Makes complete sense to me! If you're not moving forward, then you're falling behind.

Sometimes, what seems obvious to some isn't clear to others. Work with your employees to create a career plan that allows them to see what their career path looks like in your organization. Make sure the next step isn't too far out. I was recently speaking with a senior executive of a Fortune 500 company who explained his three-to-five-year succession plan for his directors. When he was done, I pointed out that it was highly unlikely his people would be around three years from now if he didn't accelerate his plan. This holds especially true for workers who make in excess of $100,000 a year.

According to a new report from Ladders, a leader in the professional job search industry, most workers who make more than $100,000 are planning to quit their jobs within a year.[3] Ladders surveyed more than 50,000 workers earning over six figures and found that 67 percent of these workers see themselves at a different company in just six months. In an article posted on CNBC titled "67% of Workers Earning Over $100,000 See Themselves Quitting in the Next Six Months—Here's Why," written by Abigail Hess, Ladders CEO Marc Cenedella is quoted as saying, "The gold rush of 2019 is on. With an incredibly strong employment market, more professionals than ever are on the lookout for a better future." Employers need to take action today, to prevent a mass exodus tomorrow.

It's important to understand that not all opportunities need to come in the form of a promotion. Companies can provide employees opportunities for additional exposure and personal growth by offering team members the chance to participate in mentoring or coaching programs, and encouraging employees to attend industry meetings and conferences. Employers can also establish employee rotation programs, where employees learn new skills while gaining exposure to other parts of the organization. Global companies can also provide employees with an opportunity to live and work internationally.

If you work in a small business or a flat organization and are unable to offer your people these options, don't despair. You can offer employees the opportunity to spend the day with a member of the executive team. This will allow employees to experience what it's like to work at a higher level, giving them exposure they would not normally have. Give people a chance to present at the next all-staff meeting. Debrief after the meeting to point out all the things your employee did well and to offer suggestions for their next presentation. The next time you visit a customer, bring an employee with you. The experience of spending an afternoon with the boss and a key client will be one your employee will remember for years to come.

Autonomy

Employers tend to throw money at employee morale problems, but what workers really want is freedom from micromanagement. Employees want to make decisions themselves without having to run everything up the ladder or needing to submit endless proposals to a committee for final approval. Autonomy makes workers feel more in control of their own responsibilities and less vulnerable to the opinions of others. Often, the people doing the micromanaging know less about the work than the actual employee.

If you are doing a great job in terms of employee selection, then giving team members autonomy shouldn't be problematic. That's why I advise my clients to be highly selective when filling positions—even if that means a job remains vacant longer than they might like. If you have a stellar team and you're micromanaging them, then the problem is you. Granting autonomy only becomes an issue when you bring on less than exceptional talent.

Micromanagement is about lack of trust. Those who micromanage believe that no one can do the job as well as they can. At some point, you have to let go and allow your people to do what you hired them to do. If you can't handle relaxing control, soon there will be no one left on your team. Then you'll have plenty of opportunity to do your employees' work as well as your own!

Flexibility

The workplace has become incredibly demanding, leaving employees little time for themselves. Employees crave flexibility at work.

I can relate to this, as my generation is part of the sandwich generation. We raised our kids while working *and* while being caregivers to aging parents. We managed all of this without going over our allotted two weeks of vacation time. Crazy? Yes. Would I recommend this lifestyle to others? Heck, no! We fooled people (and ourselves) into thinking we were able to do it all. In reality, something had to give. Turns out, that something was usually the quality of our work, our productivity, or our personal lives. You may not see a direct correlation between an employee's personal life and your bottom line, but trust me, there is one.

Over the past decade, we've seen a shift in the way work gets done. Technology has made it possible to work from almost anywhere. Managers can quickly pull together global team members through conferencing software such as Skype or Zoom. Leaders are becoming more comfortable letting go of the management style that needs to see employees in order to know they are working.

Organizations with personnel practices that give employees the ability to set their own hours and work remotely are in a much better position to attract and retain talent than those who don't. In fact, many employees will actually choose flexible schedules over pay!

Interesting Work

Imagine going to work every day, sorting the mail, and then filing paperwork for the next eight hours. I don't have to imagine it because this was my first "real" job. I worked full time as a file clerk in a law firm, and I quickly understood where the term "going postal" came from. I knew I couldn't remain in that role for very long. I lasted a year, and by the time I was done, I couldn't wait to return to college.

Not every job can be thrilling all the time. However, I do believe things can usually be done to make even the most boring work a bit more interesting. When designing jobs, consider ways to make the work challenging. Don't know what this might look like? No problem. Ask employees currently in those jobs for their suggestions. Whenever possible, mix things up. Encourage workers to rotate into more challenging jobs when there are opportunities to do so.

Before creating new positions, consider which of your people might be interested in challenging themselves by taking on new tasks. If need be, include some of this employee's current responsibilities in the new position you are creating.

Evergreen Employee Development Framework

The talent shortage isn't going away anytime soon, and now you know what employees are looking for. With that in mind, let's turn our attention to what steps you can take to grow and sustain your own talent. This is what evergreen talent is really about. Let's begin.

Assessing Talent

Remember when you were in elementary school and your teacher did a full review of information you already knew for the benefit of a few people who didn't get the concept the first time around? It was maddening, wasn't it? Well, the same thing happens every day in corporate America. Organizations are offering broad training initiatives with the hopes that their solution will help the many. In fact, to avoid employees enrolling in learning initiatives that are not suited for them, they should target the few who will really benefit from the specific solution they are presenting. They may physically check in for the training, but mentally, their mind is elsewhere. Even worse? These employees may let others know that the training they are about to attend is a complete waste of time.

Instead, before designing training solutions, assess the development needs of individuals and the organization. By doing so, management can make informed decisions about the best ways to address competency gaps among individual employees, specific job categories, or groups/teams. Start with my four-step assessment.

Step 1: Identify the business outcomes you are trying to achieve. Where's the business heading in the next two to three years? What is the end result the employee, manager, or executive team is trying to accomplish? Will employee development contribute to this accomplishment? If the answer to the last question is no, then look at organizational issues that would be best addressed through another means—for example, through goal clarification, reorganizing or realigning a department, or working to improve employee engagement.

Step 2: Perform a gap analysis. Assess the current state of departments' or employees' performance or skills, and compare this to the desired level. The difference between the existing state

and the desired state is the gap. You can gather this information in a number of ways. Some of these include reexamining
employee performance reviews, sitting down individually with
employees, focus groups, direct manager observations, conversations with clients/customers, surveys, and self-assessments.

Step 3: Prioritize options. No doubt, a number of areas will
show up as needing improvement. Take a look at what options will
give you the most return for your investment, and start there. If
you're a manufacturing firm, your focus may be on safety training.
A company that operates in a very competitive environment might
decide sales coaching is where they need to begin and end.

Step 4: Create your plan and take action. You know what
needs to happen to move things forward. It's time to take action.
Consider if you have the subject matter expertise and the capacity
to handle your development needs in-house, or if you would be
better served by bringing in an outside expert. What approach will
work best given your objectives, company culture, and budget?
Consider the following ideas.

Employee Development Ideas for All Budgets

I work with clients of all sizes and across all industries, and I can
tell you definitively that there is no one right way to develop your
people. In many cases, how much you invest has little to do with
the results you achieve. It's really about the organization's commitment to developing and nurturing their people. You have to continually invest in people if you expect them to keep up with the
growing needs of your organization. Let's look at a few ideas to get
you started.

Employee rotation programs. This is one of my favorite
ideas, as it allows people to grow where they are planted. Employees don't have to leave the organization to try something new and
to expand their skills. Many larger organizations have formal rotation

programs. However, this can be done on an informal basis, regard-less of company size.

One of my midsize clients shared a story with me about an employee who thought he wanted to move into a marketing role. The one thing that was holding him back was the idea that if he didn't enjoy the work, he'd have to leave the company. My client solved this problem by telling the employee that he could rotate into the marketing position for a six-month period.

Furthermore, my client guaranteed this employee that he would have the option to return to his previous role at the end of the six-month rotation, should he dislike the new role. Turns out, market-ing wasn't this guy's thing. When his rotation was up, he happily returned to his position in operations.

Then, something interesting happened. Back on the ground in operations, this employee began to make sug-gestions on ways to do his job differently. You see, while working in marketing, the employee gained a much clear-er understanding of the needs of the organization's target cus-tomer. This employee was now in the perfect position to delight customers, thanks to the experience he gained working elsewhere in the company.

Association meetings and conferences. There's a lot to be learned at industry association meetings and conferences—not to mention the great networking opportunities these events af-ford those in attendance. Have your employees research upcoming events, and ask them to provide you with a brief summary of what they hope to gain by attending. If your budget is tight, limit the search to local events.

Employee book clubs. What I love about employee book clubs is that members attend because they want to—not because they have to. This is how employee book clubs work. The chairper-son of the book club works with a committee or their members and chooses the books that people will read. The company usually pays for the books. Those that want to double down on the learning may invite authors in to speak about their work. A more budget-minded approach would be to start a lending library with several copies of popular nonfiction books that are purchased by the company. Then, employees are invited to borrow these books to read at their leisure.

Lunch and learn. So many companies these days are offering free meals as perks to get employees to stay. Why not add a dash of learning to spice things up? I've been invited to facilitate conversations at lunch and learns in organizations of all sizes. The one thing they all have in common is the participants' hunger for knowledge. Sometimes, authors will waive their speaking fees if the organization purchases books for all of their attendees. Can't afford to buy everyone lunch? No problem. Some companies host lunch and learns where employees brown bag their lunches. Employees appreciate opportunities to come together and learn from an outside expert, regardless of the actual meal. They will thank you no matter which approach you take.

Individual coaching. I've coached hundreds of individuals who were looking to grow their skills and their careers. I have to say, individual coaching is by far one of the most effective ways to support employee growth. When you tap an employee on the shoulder and ask if that person would like to work with a coach, you signal that you believe your employee is worthy of your investment. I've yet to see an employee say no to an offer like this. That's because the stigma of having a coach—which used to be for remedial purposes only—has gone away. Most employees today will gladly tout the fact that they are working with a coach. It's become somewhat of a status symbol.

Individual coaching is so effective because employees receive individual attention, and they have the opportunity to work on issues that are top of mind. The focus is on creating behavioral changes. The end result of a successful coaching engagement for employees is personal growth and more career opportunities within the organization. Most become even more valuable to the organization as a result of this one-on-one guidance.

Group coaching. While individual coaching is certainly optimal, the reality is that not every organization can afford to hire personal coaches for all those who would benefit. Group coaching is an affordable way to help employees fine-tune their skills. Some companies form groups that consist of workers in similar stages in their career, while others choose to pull together employees facing similar challenges, such as those needing to improve their presentation skills. Groups may meet in person or virtually, and they often provide individuals with some one-on-one time with the facilitator.

Online learning. Online learning is all the rage these days, with LinkedIn leading the charge. This approach to learning is a great way for employees to participate in training on their own schedule.

No budget? No problem. As I mentioned earlier, MOOCs are free online courses available to anyone who enrolls. A word of caution: There are many benefits to classroom-based learning, interacting in person with colleagues, and being able to ask instructors for further clarification when needed. This approach to development may not be everyone's cup of tea.

Classroom learning. Call me old-fashioned, but given the choice, I'd choose classroom learning over virtual learning any day. That's because I learn as much from my classmates as I do from the instructor. Although virtual learning platforms attempt to replicate the live classroom dynamics, most don't come close. It makes economic sense for large companies to offer on-site classroom learning to their employees. If your organization is too small to do so, consider sending select employees to public workshops when there is a class that is a good fit for their developmental needs.

Compressed learning. I experienced the benefit of compressed learning firsthand when GetAbstract chose to include my books in their extensive library. Companies like GetAbstract create summaries of popular nonfiction books that are similar to those found on the website CliffsNotes (if you're like me, you might have relied heavily on these CliffsNotes summaries in high school and college!). This approach to development is perfect for the time-starved learner. Naturally, readers won't learn everything the writer has to say about a particular topic. However, they will walk away with an understanding of the main points the author is presenting. Individuals, team members, and enterprise organizations can choose the subscription plan that is right for them. There are a number of companies in the compressed learning space. Google around, and compare your options.

Author dinners. The idea of hosting an author for dinner and inviting members of your management team to attend might sound like something only those in Hollywood can afford to do. Rest assured, it's not actually as difficult—or expensive—as you might think. Arrange an event like this, and you will feed both the bodies and souls of your leaders.

Commercially published authors need to sell books if they ever want to receive another book deal—and most authors are open to doing whatever is necessary to publicize their books. I've been invited to dine (whether it be dinner or breakfast) with executive teams, to help them stretch their thinking on matters related to talent. The intimate gathering of sharing a meal is beneficial to both author and attendees. Reach out to an author who is releasing a new book, and you'll see that most will be open to dining with your team for a modest fee. Buy enough books, and they may even do so for free. You get the bragging rights, your employees get a once-in-a-lifetime experience, and authors walk away feeling satisfied that their messages are being heard by those who can benefit from it.

Tuition assistance. College is expensive these days. Many workers who need to improve their skills would like to return to school. Employees may want to further their education, but often they can't afford to do so. That's where you come in. Tuition assistance programs, where employees are reimbursed for successfully completing college-level coursework, have become the norm. Companies like Starbucks and Disney are leading the way by extending their tuition assistance programs to their part-time workers. These companies are raising the bar for others.

In particular, if you are asking employees to return to school to raise their skill levels, then you need to be prepared to help them do so. Determine what you can afford to invest in terms of tuition reimbursement. *Remember, something is always better than nothing.*

Why One-Size-Fits-All Training Fits No One

When my daughter was in her early teens, we went shopping at Brandy Melville. The store was packed with young women of all sizes trying on the same clothes, which were marked OS (one size). At first I thought this sizing was clever, as the company was doing its part to fight negative body image—which comes naturally when your friends are grabbing size zero garb and you're into the double-digits. Then my daughter tried on clothes while I observed from the sidelines. People exited the fitting rooms, looking for approval from friends and family members. I remember silently thinking, "No one looks good in these clothes." That's because in their effort to serve everyone in a democratic fashion, this company failed to take into consideration that their customers were individuals.

I see a similar thing happening in organizations when they try to apply one-size-fits-all approach to training and development. People are squeezed into these sessions with the hope that they'll come out in better condition than when they started. Sadly, this is not the case. Employees become dismayed and then reticent about attending future sessions. I can't say I blame them.

Research shows that people learn differently. That's why I encourage clients to offer different delivery options, when possible, in terms of learning and development. For example, auditory learners prefer to hear information. These types of learners may benefit from a training program that involves listening to podcasts or audio books. In contrast, visual learners are partial to seeing and observing things. They may learn best with hands-on training and visual aids. It will take some trial and error before you get this right. At the end of the day, the goal of employee training is to empower your people to complete their tasks more effectively through new knowledge and skills. This is an important outcome—so take your time, and ask people what they need in order to learn best.

Busting Myths Regarding Employee Development

There are as many myths about employee development as there are vendors offering to take this task off your hands. In the interest of time, we'll debunk six of the most common myths.

Myth 1: Young people only want to learn online. If that were true, there would be no more brick-and-mortar colleges and universities. Like their older colleagues, learning styles of younger workers vary. Just because many are tech wizards doesn't mean they'd all prefer to learn from a screen. Take the time to get to know the learning style of the people you manage, regardless of their age. Then adapt your delivery accordingly.

**Myth 2: Mature workers have very little interest in em-
ployee development.** Boston College recently published a report
from their Center on Aging and Work, entitled "The Three Things
Employers Need to Know About: Training and Development for
Workers 50+." This report highlights that eight out of ten workers aged forty-five to sixty-four say that the opportunity to learn
something new is an essential element of their ideal job. And more
than seven out of ten of these workers also rate on-the-job training
as a critical component of a desirable career.

Myth 3: Talent development only makes sense for new hires.
This training is different than what established workers need.
However, the two are not mutually exclusive. Providing training
exclusively to new hires, and then doing nothing to nurture these
employees over the long haul, is extremely counterproductive.
This is a lot like planting award-winning roses and then never wa-
tering them. In both cases, the end result will certainly be nothing
to brag about.

Myth 4: Employee development will happen on its own.
And yes, your children will become well-rounded adults with little
effort on your part. Both statements are wrong. Employees may
want to better themselves, but many don't know the steps necessary to do so. That's why I recommend that my clients create individual development plans, including career plans, for *all* employees. This approach to performance improvement makes growth a
shared responsibility—which is ideally what it should be.

Myth 5: Talent development is costly. Actually, not doing talent development is what can cost you dearly. You may lose valuable employees to the competition, who are willing to invest in
their people. Unwanted employee turnover (up to three times an
employee's annual earnings) is expensive and should be avoided
at all costs. You may be putting your revenues at risk, as well as your
company's reputation, when clients take their business elsewhere

after receiving subpar service. Business growth comes to a halt when you no longer have the skilled workforce you need to move your company forward.

Myth 6: If you educate people, they will just wind up leaving. That may be true. But what if you don't educate your workforce, and those people choose to stay? Do you really want them representing your company, interacting with your customers, and tarnishing your employer brand? It's my experience that if you invest in your people and you treat them well, they'll feel more loyal. These employees will actually be less likely to leave if you provide them with development than if you do nothing.

Applying the Knowledge

As you look to grow talent internally, consider the following:

- What do workers in your industry really want from their employers? (Hint: Don't know? Ask recent hires why they decided to come work for you.)

- What are some methods you will use to assess development needs in your organization? Who will be responsible for this?

- From the list provided, which two or three employee development ideas will you look into implementing in your organization? Write this down, along with the date you are targeting for implementation. Take this one step further, by working backward and breaking down the steps necessary to achieve your objectives. Note target dates for each step.

- Which employee development myth(s) are you guilty of contributing to? What will you commit to doing differently to change your thinking about how you approach employee development in your organization?

9.

Replenishing Talent: Ensuring Your New Crop of Talent Takes Root

E ventually, *everyone* will leave their organization. Some may retire, be fired, or depart to pursue other opportunities. Organizations need to be ready to replenish talent at a moment's notice.

You need to get really good at attracting and hiring people. However, your efforts cannot stop there. I've seen way too many organizations rest on their laurels after making job offers, only to find that people are changing their minds. It's not uncommon to find that sometime between when an offer is accepted and an employee's start date, a person will decide to go with a better offer. Let's make sure this doesn't happen to you.

Preemployment Engagement

It's the Wild West out there in terms of talent, as ethics have been pushed aside and replaced by desperate moves to secure the best people at all costs. No longer is it considered inappropriate to poach talent, nor is it wrong to steal people who haven't even begun employment with their new employers. Thanks to social media, it's easy to see who is moving around. An announcement on LinkedIn or Facebook that someone is leaving their current employer signals to others that this individual is fair game. Let's look at some steps you can take to ensure that those you've hired, do in fact join your organization.

Stay in touch. I get the fact that many are filling multiple jobs on their teams, and these leaders may be feeling relieved that they've got one less opening to worry about. However tempting it may be, this is *not* the time to kick back and place your focus elsewhere. An occasional phone call, text, or quick email will go a long way to engage candidates who have accepted your offer. Send a message to let your new hires know how excited you are to have them on your team. You may even consider inviting new employees to attend a team meeting virtually, prior to their start date. Take this opportunity to introduce your new person to the rest of the team, and ask for their input on a few key items. The idea here is to make employees feel like they are already part of the team and to signal to them how excited you are about their arrival.

Engaging family and friends. It seems like every opinion counts these days. Young people are open about seeking advice from their parents regarding their career decisions. Parents are often involved with Gen Z and sometimes Millennial's decisions as well. With that in mind, consider including family members and friends when preengaging employees.

Invite new employees to company social events that are taking place before their start date, and add a plus-one so they can bring a friend or a family member along. (By the way, this is a great recruiting tool too. Guests of your new employees may be so impressed that they apply for a job with your organization as well.)

This strategy is inexpensive, and can go a long way in reeling in Millennial talent. Simply acknowledging the importance of parents in these workers' lives will help you stand out from other companies.

Ideas for Preboarding New Hires

If you've traveled by air recently, then you know how demeaning the preboarding process can be. First-class passengers and members with certain status in an airline's frequent-flyer program are invited to board through a special roped-off area that's nicely carpeted. Next come military personnel and those traveling with small children, followed by those who've purchased more leg room. The gate agent then closes the special boarding area and opens up the adjacent roped area for the third-class citizens, also known as coach passengers, to board. It's a horrific system, which is in need of a complete overhaul. I see a similar thing happening in organizations, in terms of how companies onboard executives versus rank-and-file personnel.

Newly hired executives have the red carpet rolled out for them, while at the same time, new workers are lucky if someone remembers to put down the welcome mat before they arrive. An executive's first day usually includes lunch at a five-star restaurant, while other newly hired employees are welcomed with a sandwich from a local sub shop. Some rank-and-file employees don't even get that.

For advice on this topic, I turned to some companies that are doing this well. Admittedly, they got to this place through trial and error. Perhaps sharing their stories will help you to get to where you need to be faster, and with less stress and drama.

Stephanie Troiano is the marketing manager for The Hire Talent, a prehire assessment testing company that is focused on helping businesses, CEOs, and HR teams hire better quality candidates. The Hire Talent helps companies do this through the use of tools, interview training, and best hiring and recruitment process consulting. Troiano says,

> When hiring new people, we tend to keep the lines of communication open with them from the time we decide we want to offer them the position until they start

with us—and even after! When we extend an offer and the candidate accepts, we immediately get the candidate set up with a company email account. We then send the new employee any important documents, like a training guide, job description, and any ancillary resources new hires should have at their disposal when starting with us. Typically, we assign a couple books to read when new hires start. We'll get them set up with hard copies or e-book versions of these books, so employees can get a head start on the readings if they wish. If new candidates don't start right away, we keep in touch with them via phone and email to continue to pulse check their interest level. We want to make sure that our new hires are engaged throughout the process, as well as after they start.

Another company that has mastered the art of engaging employees before they start work is *Murfie.com*. This company offers a high-fidelity music streaming and collection management platform, headquartered in Madison, Wisconsin. CEO Rex Mangat has found that engaging candidates early *and* creatively is a must for his company to be successful at attracting and hiring the best talent.

We tried a few things that didn't resonate but started to see great success with music-related activities. Over time, we've developed what we refer to as "the red carpet treatment."

Our first priority is to get new employees engaged with their team, so we assign an onboarding mentor to help acclimate them to their department culture. We want to make new hires feel like they're already a part of the team—without being overwhelming. The onboarding mentor is a single point of contact for all the new hire's questions and concerns. Usually, this isn't an HR rep but an adjacent contemporary.

Secondly, we want to accelerate the administrative aspects of new employee onboarding, and get these employees to start thinking long term as early as possible. This includes having new hires consider their 401(k) contributions, etc.— making these elections from the outset with the help of HR.

We encourage early and consistent collaboration with future teammates by having new hires curate their teams' weekly playlists, and having them take a music personality quiz that staff members find entertaining. We help new employees personalize their workspaces early on through a series of conversations. The point is to make them feel like they already have a space and place to call their own within our company. We also begin to make these new people aware of the projects they will be working on.

Finally, we encourage new employees to stay in contact throughout the process. We ask our hires to be transparent and to let us know if they're fielding other offers. We let these people know that we don't mind if there is some competition over them, as talent in the Midwest is hard to come by. However, this mutual transparency allows us to keep our offer fluid and competitive.

A year ago, we would lose almost half of candidates in the offer process. Now, we barely lose any.

Here are more ideas to engage new hires *before* they arrive.

Treat every employee like an executive. Roll out the red carpet the moment an employee says yes to your offer. Allow them to board your organization through the fast lane. This means answering calls or emails from them within four hours whenever possible. Streamline your new hire process, so they can complete forms online prior to their first day of work. Assign a company ambassador to help shepherd them as they navigate their way to the first day of work in your organization. Go all out on an employee's first day. Clear your calendar so you can take newly hired employees out for lunch. And if your budget permits, invite members of the team to join you.

Get social. Chances are, most newly hired employees are on social media. Ask for permission to share the exciting news about their move to your organization on your company's social network. Signal how excited you are to have the new person on your team. Worried about potential poachers seeing this information? You don't have to be, if you are incorporating some of the ideas I'm presenting into your preboarding process. What you are doing here is painting a picture for the employee to see. Newly hired employees will begin to envision themselves as part of your team. This is exactly what's needed to help ensure that your incredible new hire no longer continues to entertain other offers after accepting a position with your company.

Video messages from team members. Video is a great tool to connect newly hired employees with the rest of the team. Encourage team members to send brief videos from their phones to let new hires know how excited they are to work with them. If you can get the group together, that's great! If not, a couple of heartfelt welcome messages from individuals will suffice. If you want to take this up a notch, have an executive send a personalized video greeting to the new hire. Receiving a video from someone that new hires might think would have limited interest in their onboarding could go miles in terms of making them feel immediately valued. If your company is small enough, you can even have the CEO do this as well!

Swag bag. Who doesn't like free company-branded gifts? Put together a company swag bag, and send this to the home of new hires who have just accepted your job offer. When assembling swag bags, consider what would be most appealing to your new hire. Think quality over quantity. I'm sure you've been the recipient of a complimentary branded item in the past that has found its way into your trash barrel directly after you received it. Avoid these types of gifts. Branded phone chargers, tickets to a nearby attraction, a gift certificate to the local gym, or a branded coupon for a mental health day are just a few good ideas to get you started. Best-case scenario? Your corporate hoodie attracts so many compliments that new talent wants to flock to your organization just to get one!

Celebration gift card. Imagine receiving an American Express gift card from your new employer, along with a note encouraging you to take a friend or your family out to celebrate your new job. How cool would that be? I bet you would tell lots of people about this, and would most likely share photos of your dining experience for all to see. Of course, when doing so, you'd mention that your new employer picked up the tab! Did someone say additional marketing for your employer brand?

Onboarding for Transplanted Employees

If you've ever transferred to a new department or a new division, then you've probably experienced what it's like to be an Amazon package. Upon arrival, the receptionist has you wait in an assigned area until your new boss retrieves you. You wait patiently for your new boss to claim you, looking up hopefully and expectantly at those who pass by. For the lucky ones, your new supervisor may appear immediately. For others, several hours might go by until they are retrieved. Surely, there's a better way to integrate transplanted employees into their new roles.

There's no point in reinventing the wheel. Many of the ideas outlined for the welcoming of prehires can be applied to the welcoming of transplanted employees as well. In addition to the ideas presented, I recommend assigning a buddy to help newly trans-ferred employees quickly take root. A seasoned team member can keep employees grounded, particularly during the transition phase. Like the older redwoods providing shelter for the new seed-lings, these veteran employees can thrash through the blockage that often leaves transplanted employees second-guessing their decision to make the move to their new home.

Keeping the Bloom on the Rose Long After the Growing Season Has Passed

Have you noticed how some people's roses bloom longer than others? I have. That's probably because the roses in my garden flame out way before my neighbors' roses. Admittedly, I do nothing to cultivate my roses. Nevertheless, I'm always surprised when this happens.

I see a similar pattern occur in organizations. Employees who blossom on their own are left unattended. Eventually they wither, which shocks their employer. Employers have no idea how this happens. Or do they?

My guess is that most employers do know, especially those who conduct annual employee engagement surveys. Survey results consistently show that employees want to be developed. In their quest to increase their engagement scores, employers will add training programs. In less sophisticated organizations, this is done with little research into exactly what kind of training employees need and value most.

It's not as complicated as those big companies who sell em-ployee engagement surveys would like you to believe.

Matuson's Evergreen Talent 30-60-90 Cultivator

I'm about to share with you a concept that I've coined "Matuson's Evergreen Talent 30-60-90 Cultivator." Get your highlighters out, as this is something you are going to want to deploy in your organization. Here we go.

Ask newly hired employees the following questions when they reach their thirty-, sixty-, and ninety-day marks of employment. It's best to do this in person. If this isn't possible, then consider using video conferencing technology. You want to be able to pick up on nonverbal cues.

30 DAYS	60 DAYS	90 DAYS
Is the job what you expected it to be? If not, what's different?	What areas of your job are you enjoying most? The least?	What were your hopes when you took this job? Are you still hopeful that you'll be able to accomplish what you came here to do?
What training or resources do you need from me to be successful in your role?	What skills, if any, would you like to develop and strengthen in the upcoming weeks and months?	How can I help you feel more connected in the organization? Who would it be helpful to meet?
Are there any challenges in particular that I can assist you with?	What can I do to best support you?	Would you recommend us as an employer to a friend or relative? If not, what needs to change for you to say yes without hesitation?

I've kept this simple so you can focus your efforts on having *meaningful* conversations. Feel free to flip these questions around or add a few of your own.

Buddy Up to Bolster New Employees

Most people don't have fond memories of their first few days or months of work. In an effort to make a great first impression with our bosses, we pretend we know more than we do. Imagine how much more productive and less stressed out we'd be if all new hires were assigned an individual to help them through the transition. There are a number of companies that do this. Each new hire is assigned a work buddy who is there to show them the ropes. They operate in a similar capacity to the stakes we use when growing tomatoes. They can be leaned on while new employees get rooted, and provide support as needed.

When selecting buddies, consider the following:

Reach out to experienced strong performers. Pick employees who are knowledgeable and who best represent your organization's values. You don't want people who will teach new staff bad habits.

Make sure they are accessible. A buddy who works a different shift or who is housed at a different location won't be much help to an employee in need of immediate assistance. Be careful not to select employees who are often called away on assignments for this role.

Choose buddies who are good at teaching others. There are people who are good at what they do and not so great at teaching others. You want to steer clear of these individuals. Look for people who can explain procedures in a way that others can understand.

Manage expectations. Buddies are volunteers and generally do not receive additional compensation for working in this capacity. Monitor the workload of buddies to ensure that they are not overloaded, and check to make sure they are not taking on the role of the supervisor.

Acknowledge buddies for their added contribution in helping transition in your new employees. Enter them into a drawing for a gift, treat them to lunch, or offer some new company swag as a thank you for their volunteer efforts.

Engage New Employees in the Recruitment Process

Who better to get prospective employees excited about an organization than those who have recently joined? Take a page out of the college recruitment playbook. Colleges and universities heavily rely on students to sing the praises to new recruits. Having just completed three years of college touring with two teenagers in tow, I can attest to the effectiveness of this strategy.

Here's how to engage new recruits in your hiring process:

Learn from new recruits. Being asked for advice goes a long way in terms of engaging new employees—or any employee, for that matter. Listen carefully, as these new employee insights can help you dramatically improve your ability to attract and hire even more talent. Some questions to ask include: What initially drew you to our organization? Why did you ultimately decide to come work for our company? What can we do better in terms of our recruitment process?

Include new recruits in your future recruitment process. When doing so, give these employees the tools they need to be effective. This includes access to recruitment marketing materials, and training on how to effectively network to attract new team members. If you are asking newly hired employees to participate in recruitment events, then make sure they understand what their role is and how they fit into the bigger picture. Pair these workers up with someone who has experience in the recruitment process, so they can quickly learn the ropes.

Teach new recruits how to select for success. There's nothing worse than the feeling you get when you know you're in over your head. Your confidence is rattled, and it shows. That happens a lot when people are asked to conduct interviews without any formal training. If you're going to have new hires participate in the company recruitment and hiring process, you need to be ready to train these people on how to interview and assess candidates. By offering this training, you'll ensure that new employees quickly become valuable members of your hiring team.

Training New Recruits on How to Recognize and Select Evergreen Talent

I could write a whole book on teaching new recruits how to identify evergreen talent. However, in the interest of space, here are a couple of guidelines you can use to begin training your new hires to select for success.

The Ten Questions You Need to Ask Before Hiring Anyone

People are in such a rush these days to fill job openings that many have lost sight of what's most important regarding hiring. As a result, they're hiring the wrong people. This creates unnecessary employee churn—and chaos, which comes with high levels of employee turnover. You can avoid this by asking yourself the right questions before extending a job offer.

Here are the ten questions you need to ask before hiring anyone:

1. What outcomes do I expect this person to achieve, and does he have the skills to do what I need him to do?

2. Do I have the time that's needed to help develop this person?

3. What are the person's goals, and are they in alignment with the actual position we are considering her for?

4. Will this candidate be able to grow with our organization?

5. Is this person answering questions honestly, or is he simply telling me what I want to hear?

6. Is this person the right fit for my team?

7. How long will this person be happy in this role before seeking other opportunities?

8. Is this person's behavior during the interview in alignment with what they're saying?

9. Is this person looking for *a job with our company,* or are they simply looking for *a job?*

10. Is this person good enough, or am I settling?

Common Red Flags When Hiring Someone

When it comes to costly workplace mistakes, few carry as hefty of a price tag as making a wrong hire. According to press release issued by CareerBuilder in December of 2017, a study found that nearly three in four employers (74 percent) say they've hired the wrong person for a position. Here are some warning signs you are about to make a hiring mistake.

Late arrival. If a person is late to what most would consider an important meeting, it doesn't bode well for how prompt they'll be for work—or for an important meeting with a client. Keep in mind that most employees put their best foot forward during the interview process. If this is as good as it gets, then things will most likely go downhill from here. Don't say you haven't been forewarned.

Missing interviews. Candidates who continually reschedule or miss interviews are demonstrating that they are disorganized and unreliable. How likely do you think it is that this behavior will change, should you decide to hire them? My guess is, not likely.

Resume errors. It's easy to make a mistake or two, thanks to autocorrect. But what if a person's resume is filled with typos? This would indicate to me that a candidate lacks attention to detail. I would pass on this person, especially if the job they are applying for requires a ton of written communication!

Arriving unprepared. Does the candidate look like a deer in headlights when you ask the question, "What do you know about our company?" Blank stares, or the blurting out of a few well-known facts, indicate this person has not done their homework. In this day and age of mobile devices and Internet access, there is no good excuse for a candidate showing up unprepared. If they haven't taken the time to learn more about you, then why are you spending more time learning about them?

Lies. I've busted enough candidates to know that lies are quite common during the interview process. In particular, candidates who have attended a university but haven't completed their education are masters at giving the illusion that they are graduates of the institution they are describing. If you suspect someone is lying, probe a bit more. Ask the same question more than once, but in different ways. If you get different answers, then you know the person in front of you isn't trustworthy. Statements that are commonly exaggerated include scope of responsibility, most recent salary, latest performance evaluation rating, credentials, and skill embellishment.

Ambiguous answers. You ask a question and are given a vague answer. You follow up by asking, "Can you give me an example?" The candidate responds with another vague answer. This person either isn't one for the details or is bluffing. In either case, I'd recommend taking a pass.

Lack of enthusiasm. You can't fake enthusiasm. If a candidate isn't getting excited about the position she is interviewing for, then what do you think will happen the moment she lands the job? I can assure you she won't be walking into work each day, excited about what the day may bring. Keep interviewing. You'll find someone who is both qualified *and* excited about the position you are looking to fill.

Negativity. This is the candidate who blames his failures on everyone but himself. During the interview, he tells you about his terrible manager and his lazy coworkers at his last company. If you ignore this and hire him, it will only be a matter of time before he says the same thing about you to anyone who will listen.

No questions. Even my teenage daughter knows enough to go into an interview with some questions for when the interviewer says, "So, do you have any questions for me?" Maybe all of the candidate's questions were answered during the interview. However, this is the perfect opportunity for candidates to show potential employers that they can think on their feet while demonstrating interest in the position.

Too many questions. Of course, the opposite can happen when you ask a candidate if he has any questions, and he shoots off a barrage of questions that are more about him than about the organization. Think about the following questions: "How much will I be paid, and when will I be eligible for a salary increase?" "When will I get my own office?" "When will I get promoted so I don't have anyone telling me what to do?" Questions like these may signal that the candidate is more interested in what he can get out of the organization, rather than what he can contribute to the company.

Unexplained gaps in employment. These days, it's fairly common for job seekers to have gaps in their resumes due to sabbaticals, taking time off to care for family members, etc. It's candidates who seem unable to explain exactly where they've been for a long period of time that are most concerning. Probe further. If the response you receive seems too out of the box, then be prepared to move on.

Upfront demands. Candidates who walk in with a demand list as long as one you expect from a rock star might be signaling to you that they are divas. Demands like, "I need a reserved parking space," "I can only work the third and fourth Monday of every month," or "I need to leave by 2:59 p.m. daily to get to my yoga class" may point to candidates who could be more trouble than they are worth. No doubt they will have even more demands, should you make the decision to hire them.

Unprofessional appearance. I no longer expect most candidates to show up in a suit these days, but I do expect them to be dressed appropriately and to be well groomed. If they are not, this demonstrates to me that they are really not that invested in being hired—or perhaps they are just lazy. In either case, I'd take a pass.

They're constantly changing jobs. I get that longevity is in short supply these days, in terms of employee retention. However, someone who has a new job every few months would raise more than a few red flags for me. My advice to you is to run the other way!

Their career goals don't align with what you can offer. If someone tells you her career goal is to be a nurse, and she is applying for a sales position at a tech company, that indicates that you probably can't count on her to be a successful, long-term employee. Finding candidates with personal goals that are in alignment with the role they are applying for, as well as the mission and values of the company, is critical for retaining long-term talent.

Applying the Knowledge

As you look to replenish talent, consider the following:

¤ What two or three recommendations presented in this chapter speak to you in terms of engaging prehires? Jot down each idea, along with a date that you will commit to implementing these practices in your organization.

¤ On a scale of 1–10 (with 10 being high), how would you rate your current onboarding process? Don't know? Ask recently hired employees this question: If the number is less than a 10, what would it take for your onboarding process to become a 10?

¤ Who else in your organization needs to be involved in employee onboarding? Write down their names and departments, and invite them to participate in the process.

¤ Who in the organization is currently involved with employee onboarding that shouldn't be? Send them a note and inform them that their help is no longer required. Be sure to thank them for their past efforts.

¤ What's your process for onboarding employees who transfer to new office locations or departments? Unsure? Ask. If there is no process, what steps will you take to change this?

¤ Mark your calendar to meet individually with newly hired employees thirty, sixty, and ninety days after their start dates to ensure you are cultivating evergreen talent. Which questions from Matuson's Evergreen Talent 30-60-90 Cultivator will you ask each employee? Make a note of questions you will add to this list.

....

¤ Write down the names of people in your department or
   team that you will ask to buddy up with new employees.
   Before you need to engage them, reach out to these people
   to see if they are willing and excited to participate.

¤ What steps will you take to engage new hires in your recruitment process? How will you prepare these employees
   to take on this important role?

10.

The Canopy of Mature Workers: Why Evergreen Employees are Vital to Your Company's Survival

If you are under the age of forty and you are reading this, I have some alarming news to share. One day (if you're lucky enough to live that long), you will be a mature worker. You'll be over the age of forty, so tread lightly here. I can tell you from experience, it's not that bad. In fact, it's pretty great. The view from this vantage point is quite enlightening!

When you achieve mature worker status, experience is on your side. People assume you know what you are doing, which frees you up to operate with little supervision.

I didn't really figure out the rules of work until I was well into my thirties. Knowing what I know today makes people like me extremely valuable to organizations. I've mastered the skills needed to be successful in my role as a strategic advisor. I'm confident and fearless. And I'm not afraid to speak my mind. I may have thought I was all of this and more back in my twenties—but that just shows you how naive I was. Now, who wouldn't want a dose of someone like me in their organization?

Working Baby Boomers may be dwindling in numbers, but they are still a force to be reckoned with. According to a Pew Research Center analysis of US Census Bureau data, as of 2017, there were 41 million Baby Boomers (born 1946 to 1964) who were still actively working. That means that this generation represents a quarter of the workforce. The knowledge and experience this group of employees commands is tremendous. Companies have a great opportunity to tap this valuable resource. Don't wait too long to do so as there is no telling when they'll be gone.

Dispelling Myths Regarding Mature Workers

There are a number of myths regarding mature workers. Let's cut to the chase and dispel some of the most popular ones.

Myth 1: Older workers are waiting around for retirement. A former roommate of mine was recently asked to take on a new role in her company, which was completely out of her area of expertise. She gave it much consideration before saying yes. That's understandable, given how comfortable she was in her current role. Eventually, she agreed to take on this new challenge—and she now reports that she's glad she did. This worker has been quite energized by her new job. As a result, she once again looks forward to coming to the office every day. Not everyone is looking forward to retirement. The older workers I know still have a lot to offer, and they continue actively looking for ways to contribute at work.

Myth 2: Mature workers are not tech savvy. Assumptions like this do more harm than good. A number of my clients have told me they've encountered many mature team members who are tech savvy. Some even more so than their younger counterparts.

Myth 3: Those at the tail end of their careers have little interest in learning. Studies consistently show that employees of *all* ages highly value employee development. The desire for opportunities to learn and grow seem to be a common thread across every generation. Ensuring that training and development opportunities are open and available to *all* staff, regardless of age, is a business practice worth following.

Myth 4: If seasoned workers can't run the show, then they are not interested in participating. It seems that as you age, time is more valuable than money. I recall my days in management when I needed to burn the midnight oil in order to move up to the next rung in the organization. Thank goodness those days are gone! Many of my peers feel the same way. They've reached a point in their lives where they are fine riding in the passenger seat. They look forward to coming to work every day, doing their job well, and letting someone else run the operation. Something to consider before putting this group of employees out to pasture.

Myth 5: They're not coachable. By most standards, New England Patriots quarterback Tom Brady would be considered "past his prime." How many quarterbacks are still playing professional football at his level, at the ripe old age of forty-two? Many would argue that Brady is the best quarterback in history. Despite this, he still has people coaching him daily. I receive many inquiries from people looking to hire me for coaching. The lion's share are experienced leaders who recognize that they still have more room for growth. If Tom Brady can improve, so can the rest of us! The people who are most coachable (irrespective of age), are the ones open to making changes. As you should be able to see by now, this capacity has nothing to do with age.

Myth 6: Mature workers are inflexible. Are some mature workers set in their ways? You betcha. However, I know workers from other generations who fall into this camp as well. Just because you've encountered an older worker who is inflexible doesn't mean all older workers are like this. Keep this in mind the next time you are tempted to lump people together before getting to know them.

Myth 7: Older workers lack stamina. Really? Tell that to my client who is in her sixties and is about to climb Mt. Kilimanjaro! Sure, there are older people living life on their couch. However, there are plenty of younger people planted on their own couches, gaming into all hours of the morning. Anyone dissing rumors about their stamina? Base your evaluation regarding someone's stamina on what you see, not what you've heard.

Myth 8: They are not interested in teaching younger workers the ropes. I'd have to agree with this statement—that is, if your company is a revolving door and you're constantly asking mature workers to show less experienced employees the ropes. That would be exhausting for anyone, regardless of age. It's been my experience that mature workers enjoy mentoring up-and-coming employees who are likely to stick around. This explains why many organizations these days are implementing the kind of mentoring programs I've mentioned.

Getting Mature Workers to Stay

Employers will need to do everything in their power to keep mature workers, given the outlook for available talent. It's going to take a lot more than a hope and a prayer to make this happen. However, the good news is that it won't be as hard as you think. That is, if you start to implement some of the ideas I'm about to share with you.

Establish community. Having friends at work helps employees feel like they belong. We spend more of our waking hours at work than at home, and it's only natural that we want to build connections with people we see almost daily.

As more and more younger workers take their places at work, older workers may feel that they are no longer part of the in-crowd. That's where community comes in. Provide opportunities for workers of all ages to participate in activities that bring people together. Clubs in the workplace can be found in companies of all sizes. Some companies only offer meeting space, while other organizations actively endorse and support employee activities. Boeing sponsors about a hundred clubs, with interests as varied as making beer and wine to collecting rubber stamps to participating in book clubs. These activities are of interest to employees of all ages and abilities.

Reduced work week. Sometimes employees leave jobs because of outside family obligations that no longer make it possible to work a forty-hour week, five days a week. Giving employees the option of working a reduced work week may prevent you from losing knowledgeable and experienced workers. This option is also attractive to talented employees of all ages, who are in need of workplace flexibility.

Temp assignments. I remember reading about a consulting firm that offered several valuable employees the opportunity to take on overseas assignments on a temporary basis, prior to retirement. These employees jumped at the chance to give their lives a bit of a jolt, while still having a safety net. This sort of thinking is exactly what is needed when looking for ways to keep knowledgeable workers. You may not have an overseas office, but that doesn't preclude you from offering older workers the opportunity to take on temp assignments elsewhere in your organization. For those who are about to retire, a change of scenery might be just what they are looking for.

Snowbirding. Create passport or snowbird programs that allow employees to work in different parts of the country. Many employers, such as Home Depot and CVS, are already doing this. Employees are given the option of transferring to stores in warmer clients during the winter months and are able to return to their home base after the snow is gone. It's a win-win for both employer and employee as stores in warmer regions experience an influx of customers who are also escaping the cold. This approach can work for corporate jobs as well for those employers who are open to the idea of some part-time, remote work for their employees.

Telecommuting. I'll probably work until I'm 100 years old, as long as I can do so from the comfort of my home. There comes a time in every worker's life where the excitement of driving to and from work, with hundreds of thousands of other people, is no longer thrilling. Giving employees permission to work from home will no doubt help you keep workers much longer than if you are requiring them to come into the office daily.

Flextime. There's a lot to be said for being able to set your own hours, especially as you look to maintain your health. If you can't go all in with flextime, then consider allowing employees to choose from a range of core hours set by the company. Your flexibility, in terms of start and end times, will go a long way in helping you retain those employees who are considering other options.

Engaging Mature Workers to Foster and Grow the Next Generation of Employees

Harnessing the knowledge of experienced workers is a win-win all around, as mature workers continue to feel valued while less experienced workers get to learn firsthand from those who have already mastered their jobs. My client Mimi Brent is the former career development leader for General Motors, and she is a huge fan of mentoring and the leaders teach model. "Leveraging your experienced leaders to teach others in your organization is very effective," states Brent. "There's great value in that because you have mature workers that know the culture and know the topic. You cannot replace that with an outside instructor."

Companies that develop a culture of teaching and learning will always be in vogue. Learning organizations are more innovative. Their workers are more adaptable, which allows these companies to pivot on a moment's notice. And finally, these organizations tend to attract smart people who are always looking for ways to improve. Asking mature workers to be involved in teaching the next generation is only natural. When you do so, you'll find that most people will readily agree to participate.

Another way to leverage the experience of your mature workers is to invite them to rotate onto a team that could benefit from their knowledge. Team members will have the opportunity to learn from someone with more expertise than they have. And as a side benefit, the mature employee will most likely learn a thing or two as well. You won't have to worry about people feeling threatened when someone of this stature is brought in, because this move is temporary.

Many companies are now assembling teams in a more intentional way. They are selecting employees who offer diverse perspectives to work together on projects. This approach includes creating teams with generational diversity. One example of how this works comes from a company that put together a generationally diverse marketing team to market a product to the over-fifty set. The company made sure several team members represented their target market. They also included recent college grads who were up on the latest market-research methods. The team was rounded out by employees with experience taking new ideas to the market.

Teams composed of members with different perspectives are extremely valuable. The team diversity approach also promotes cross-generational conversations, which create a more engaged workforce for all.

Applying the Knowledge

As you look to hire and retain mature workers, consider the following:

- ¤ Which myths regarding mature workers (if any) am I guilty of buying into? What steps will I take to shift my mind-set?

- ¤ Write down the names of those mature workers whom you would really miss if they went away tomorrow. What will you do today to prevent this from happening?

- ¤ Do I have team members who have made requests related to workplace flexibility that I've declined? Which requests might I want to reconsider?

- ¤ Write down three things you can do today to make your company or department more age friendly.

- ¤ What will I do differently to create a culture of inclusiveness for all my employees?

- ¤ What am I willing to do to foster a culture of learning and development?

- ¤ Whom in the organization will I tap to be a mentor? To whom will I assign these individuals? What skills will these workers need to successfully carry out their roles as mentors, and how will I ensure they get the proper support required to be effective?

IV

Creating and Sustaining Growth

11.

Nurturing Employees to Greatness

Anyone can grow something. The question is, can they sustain this growth over time? Sustaining growth will be a key challenge when companies are no longer able to fill positions in a timely manner, and therefore, when they are unable to properly service their customers. The inability to sustain growth of internal talent will also be problematic. Top employees may go elsewhere, which leaves companies with a subpar workforce. Let's make sure you avoid this dismal fate.

The Impact Leaders Have on Growth

Leaders can help employees thrive or die. I doubt most leaders intentionally let their employees fail. They don't wake up one day saying, "I'm going to make sure that Manny doesn't succeed in his job today." It just sort of happens. Managers are busy people, especially these days. They're responsible for overseeing the workload of their assigned area, while filling in, until vacant positions are staffed.

These leaders resemble firemen trying to put out a wildfire. They are paying attention to what's burning in front of them. For many employees, this means waiting for the flames to die down before they can expect any attention. Some will wait, while others won't.

It doesn't take much time or effort to provide employees with feedback and to recognize them for their accomplishments. Many of my clients have implemented my "Time Out for a Coffee" campaign where leaders reserve time on their calendars (weekly or bi-weekly) and invite the team to join them for a coffee or tea. These informal gatherings provide an ongoing opportunity for participants to share what's on their mind. This is also a great time for leaders to acknowledge the successes of team members in front of their peers. These gatherings go a long way in terms of sparking meaningful conversations. When done right, the "Time Out for a Coffee" practice signals to employees that their boss is really interested in connecting.

As you look at your employee turnover numbers, ask yourself, "What part of the problem do I own?" Then seek help. Ask your manager for general feedback regarding your performance as a leader, and get specific advice on what you can do to improve your leadership skills. Reach out to your HR team to see if your company provides executive coaching to leaders at your level in the organization. If they say no, consider making this investment yourself.

Steps Managers Can Take to Grow Into Majestic Leaders

I know what it's like to be tossed into management with little more than a prayer. This happened to me at the ripe old age of twenty-four. I walked into work one day, only to learn that my boss had been fired the night before. When I heard the news, I did what I thought any other twenty-four-year-old would do: I asked for her job. And to my surprise, the president gave it to me! It wasn't long before I found myself in one of those sink or swim situations. In retrospect, it was a miracle that I was able to stay afloat for six years.

I learned a tremendous amount from this experience. There were times that my growth was stunted. However, in the end, I prevailed. You will as well, if you heed my advice.

Common Traits of Majestic Leaders

I've had the pleasure of working with some great leaders, many of whom I would consider majestic: they work relentlessly on their leadership skills and continue to strive for improvement. Here are some traits that majestic leaders possess:

- ¤ **Authenticity.** Majestic leaders are authentic. They don't try to be someone they are not.

- ¤ **Selflessness.** They put the needs of others in front of their own needs. They serve others before they serve themselves.

- ¤ **Innovative.** They seek ways to change the world for the better and encourage their people to do the same. They seek improvement, despite others saying it can't be done.

- ¤ **Transparency.** They don't tell people what they want to hear. They tell people what they *need* to hear. They speak the truth, even if the truth stings.

- ¤ **Resiliency.** They pick themselves back up when they've been knocked down. They push through adversity.

It's not difficult to become a majestic leader. However, sustaining majestic leadership requires a commitment to being the best version of yourself. You have to continually invest in your own development to ensure that you stand tall for years to come.

What to Do if Leaders Are Stifling Employee Growth

Sometimes leaders stifle employee growth. For example, caring too much can prevent employees from growing. Painful as it might be to see an employee struggle through a challenging task, there's a learning opportunity available within those difficult times. Leaders who try to "fix" everything so their team members face continual smooth sailing are actually robbing people of life's best teacher: failure. In the process, you may inadvertently be signaling to your team that you don't believe they are capable of handling rough waters.

Of course, there are leaders who take stifling growth to a whole other level. They closely monitor every move an employee makes. Some even go as far as assigning work, then insisting on doing the work themselves. The good news is that micromanagement is a condition, not a disease. Once leaders see how their behavior is stifling the growth of their employees—as well as their own growth— most are open to working with a coach to change their behavior. In my experience, this behavior change won't happen overnight. However, those leaders who commit to letting go of a habit that is not serving them can, and do, experience great results.

The Majestic Leadership Individual Self-Assessment

Self-reflection is something leaders should do on a regular basis. I've created a tool called the Majestic Leadership Individual Self-Assessment, so that leaders can assess where they stand. I give this to my coaching clients to help us assess their personal leadership skills.

Take a few minutes to complete this self-assessment. Then choose one or two areas that need improvement to focus on. Resist the temptation to work on the easiest skills to master. Instead, select the areas where you will realize the most growth. Any area with a score of 2 or less requires immediate attention!

Rate yourself in each of the following areas in the chart using the rating system below:

4 = All of the time
3 = Most of the time
2 = Sometimes
1 = Rarely
0 = Never
N/A = Not applicable

The Majestic Leadership Individual Self-Assessment

AUTHENTICITY	
1. I bring my whole self to work.	
2. I do something weekly to build trust.	
3. I share my backstory with employees and prospective candidates on a regular basis.	
SELFLESSNESS	
4. People follow me because of what I can do for them, rather than because of what I can do *to* them.	
5. I give more than I take.	
6. I regularly put others before myself.	

INNOVATIVENESS	
7. I frequently offer up out-of-the box ideas.	
8. I'm supportive of new ideas presented by team members and peers.	
9. I encourage my team to share their ideas with me.	
TRANSPARENCY	
10. When asked, I tell people the truth, even if it's not what they want to hear.	
11. I have an open door policy that people avail themselves of.	
12. I'm *completely* open when communicating with staff, peers, and my boss.	
RESILIENCY	
13. I take responsibility for my failures.	
14. I pick myself up quickly after a failure and move forward.	
15. I view setbacks as an opportunity to grow.	

The Connection Between Majestic Leadership and Evergreen Talent

If you have any doubt about the impact a manager has on their employees, then you'll want to read on. In a TinyPulse New Year Employee Report, 1,000 working Americans shared their workplace wishes for the New Year.[1] Participants were asked what one thing they wished they could change about their manager. *The second most popular answer was to have their manager quit.* This response aligns with what I see in my consulting practice. Leaders who grow and inspire their team members are held in much higher regard—and have considerably less employee turnover—than those who don't.

Majestic Leaders in Action

My client, Ron Bryant, is president of the Baystate Noble Hospital/ Western Region and Baystate Franklin Medical Center/Northern Region. Bryant is the type of leader others aspire to be like. He's able to attract high-quality people who are as committed to the organization as he is. Bryant is known as someone who invests in his people and supports their growth. His reputation as a leader helps secure talent for his organization at a time when most hospitals are struggling to do so. By being a majestic leader, Bryant has certainly elevated the level of care and reputation of the hospitals he oversees.

Another such leader is my client Marcus Allen, president and CEO at Big Brothers Big Sisters Independence Region. Like most nonprofit leaders, Allen doesn't have a lot of money available for employee development. However, that hasn't stopped him from helping his employees grow. Allen's leadership style is best described as charismatic. He takes an interest in his people and is there to lend a hand. Allen regularly mentors team members on an informal basis and gives them much to strive for.

Now imagine working for a leader who is more concerned with his own success than with yours. Requests for funds for employee development are quickly dismissed as "unnecessary." How long are you likely to stay with this leader? My bet is not long.

The most effective leaders I know put their employees before themselves. They understand that leadership development isn't a one-and-done kind of thing. It's an investment that pays dividends over time.

The Direct Impact Leaders Have on Employee Attraction and Turnover

Every day, employees are evaluating if they will stay with their current employer—or take their knowledge and skills elsewhere. The relationships these employees have with their managers play a big role in whether these individuals choose to stay or go. This includes how invested employees' managers are in helping them achieve their career goals. Of course, there are also those leaders who monitor every move their direct reports make and regularly give unsolicited advice. These managers are simply unable to let their people grow into well-adjusted employees.

If there are leaders like this in your organization, then it's time to take a stand. Talk to them privately about their behavior. When doing so, give them examples of what you've observed, and how their actions are being perceived. Offer to find these leaders a coach to help them break these bad habits.

Ways for Leaders to Empower Their Teams

Have you ever been in a situation where you found yourself doing the lion's share of the work? If so, then you know how exhausting this can be. It's hard to function when you are burnt out, stressed, and tired, which is how many managers feel. Life as a leader doesn't have to be this way. You have a team there to support you—that is, if you let them. Here are three actionable ways to empower you team. Try on one or two for size.

1. Shift power back to the line. When I first started out in management, frontline supervisors actually had power. They were given full responsibility for running their units. Then, somewhere along the way, programs like total quality management (TQM) were introduced, where members of an organization participate in improving processes, products, services, and the culture in which they work. Companies started forming quality circles, where groups of workers who do the same or similar work would meet regularly to identify, analyze, and solve work-related problems. While technically still in charge, supervisors and managers were suddenly beholden to their team members.

These kinds of programs have fallen out of fashion. However, their impact lives on. Many leaders continue to manage by consensus, when they should be making autonomous decisions. I don't necessarily blame the manager for this. The problem stems from top leadership failing to clearly define what is expected of first-line supervisors and managers. Leaders need to define the lines of authority for those in management positions. Decision-making responsibility should rest in the hands of those who are ultimately responsible for the results. If you're the one making the rules in your organization from the top, make sure your managers know that they have the power to act autonomously. If you're a manager who's unclear about the scope of your decision-making power, ask those who supervise you to clarify this.

2. Set expectations. I've worked for some leaders who fail to set expectations—and then wonder why expectations aren't being met. As a leader, you may think your expectations are obvious. I'm here to assure you that this is not always the case.

I'm currently working with Sue (the client's name has been changed to protect her privacy), a seasoned leader who brings tremendous value to her organization. She's thinking about giving her notice. Sue's boss has told her several times that she is disappointed in Sue's work. Yet when Sue asks for clarification, her manager is unable to tell Sue what she specifically expects in terms of performance.

Leaders need to tell their people *exactly* what they expect when it comes to performance. Continuous feedback along the way is also necessary. This way, employees can make course corrections as they go, which ultimately enables them to work more independently.

3. Sprinkle the seeds of reward and recognition. I find that most companies fall into one of two camps in terms of rewards and recognition. There are those companies where everyone is recognized and rewarded, regardless of their contribution to the company. As a result, no one is really recognized. And then there are those organizations that dole out rewards as if they were finite resources that cannot be replicated. You have to do something *really* amazing for anyone to take notice!

Come up with ideas for rewards that are meaningful to the people who will receive them. My former employer was great at doing this. The company wanted to recognize me for doing an outstanding job. Rather than hand me a check for $500—which, let's face it, wouldn't have made much of an impact—the owner paid a premium and gave me tickets to a sold-out concert that I had mentioned wanting to attend. It's been over twenty years since this happened, and I still talk about it today.

Sometimes, receiving recognition is enough. Come up with some creative award ideas to recognize stellar performance, as well as those good faith efforts. For example, you could give out an award for the best idea that didn't work. By doing so, you'll encourage others to continue to innovate—regardless of the outcome.

Identifying the Next Crop of Leaders

The current state of scarce talent also applies to available leaders. This means companies will need to grow the next crop of leaders, to ensure they have the requisite talent to successfully lead their organizations.

Once you've narrowed down your list of people who are promotable, the next step is to look at your future needs and determine who might fit where. This is called "succession planning." Most succession planning is done with a three-to-five-year horizon in mind. This is nuts, given how quickly people move in and out of organizations these days. My recommendation is to look at your talent pipeline with no more than a two-year horizon.

Let employees in on the plan. Doing so will signal to them that they have a future with your organization. Look at the skills employees will need to master so that they can be successful in their new roles. Then, work together to create a development plan. The idea is that when it comes time, these employees can step into their new jobs and be fully productive from day one.

Bolstering New Leaders

My book *Suddenly in Charge* (Nicholas Brealey, 2017) was written based on my own experience of being tossed into management without any training or support. I wrote the book because I didn't want anyone else to have to go through what I went through when I first entered management. I've since received a ton of emails from people in the same position—as well as many from their direct reports—sharing their horror stories.

Throwing someone into management is not an approach I'd recommend, especially given the frail state of the workforce. Employees have lots of options these days, so if they don't like the way they are being managed, they will quickly go elsewhere. Instead, have a support system in place for all new leaders. Let's look at some ways you can do this.

Offer management training that is specifically geared toward new leaders. Larger companies often have their own leadership training programs. Encourage new leaders to take advantage of these opportunities. If your business is on the smaller side, don't despair. Public workshops for new leaders are offered fairly frequently. Assign seasoned management mentors to new leaders. These individuals can run interference when needed, as well as provide occasional advice. Connect new leaders with a coach to ensure they start their management careers off on the right foot.

Determining If Someone Is Coachable

Suppose you are reading this book after having promoted someone who isn't quite making the grade. If that's the case, get ready to make some decisions.

I recently attended a two-day session to become certified in Marshall Goldsmith's Stakeholder Centered Coaching. Goldsmith is considered one of the world's leading executive educators, coaches, and authors. During this training, the facilitators outlined a framework to determine if someone is coachable. After hearing Goldsmith's philosophy on coaching, I became more convinced than ever that not all employees have what it takes to be coachable. I hope you will consider this before assigning someone a coach. Here are three signs that someone is *not* coachable.

1. **They aren't open to feedback.** The term "coachable" means someone is willing to be corrected, and to act on these corrections. The key word is "willing." Lots of people talk about self-improvement, but will not listen to feedback. It's impossible to help someone improve when they only want to hear what they want to hear. Save your money.

2. **They are in the wrong job.** I'm sure New England Patriots quarterback Tom Brady has some exceptional coaches. Even if I were fortunate enough to be next in line for Brady's job, there's no way these people could get me to superstar level. If we're being honest here, I'm not sure if they could even teach me how to play football. The team would be better off having me serve in a management role.

   I'm frequently asked to coach people who should never have been placed into their current job. However, many employees soar when they are moved into a job that's more suitable for their skill sets and interests. If you

have someone who you think may be in the wrong job
as a leader, take the money you were going to spend for
coaching and invest this in retooling the employee, so the
individual can move into a position in which they are better suited.

3. **You are more invested in their growth than they are.**
   You can't help people who don't want to be helped. If you
   find that you are more invested in helping your people
   grow than they are, then it's time for a reality check.

Coaching is a partnership. To be successful, both parties have
to work in concert with one another. Be honest. Is the person
you're about to assign a coach ramped up or simply going through
the motions? If it's the latter, take the money you've allocated to
this individual and funnel it to someone who is super excited to
be given an opportunity to become the best version of himself or
herself.

Applying the Knowledge

As you examine the impact your leaders have on the organization,
consider the following:

¤ Write down the names of three people in your organization who are doing a great job attracting and retaining talent. What have you noticed them doing that makes this
   possible?

¤ Make a note of the people in your organization who can't
   seem to keep people in their employ. What are they doing
   that is repelling talent? Schedule a date on your calendar
   to have a conversation with them about this. When doing so, be prepared to share specific examples of how their

behavior is impacting employee turnover. Additionally, be ready to be candid.

◻ Take the Majestic Leader Self-Assessment. How did you fare? Make a note of areas with a score of 2 or below, and create an action plan for how you will address this.

◻ Take note of those leaders in your organization whom you'd place in the Majestic Leader category. What traits do these people share?

◻ Jot down three ways you can recognize and reward employees. Make sure these strategies are realistic, and select those that fit in your budget.

◻ Write down the names of people in your workgroup who meet the criteria of being promotable into management. Take note of what skills they still need to master, so they can be fully prepared when it comes time for promotion.

◻ Write down the names of those who may have been promoted into management without it being a good fit. Are these employees better suited to a position that does not involve supervising others? If so, write down your plan for transitioning these individuals into positions that are more suited to these employees' skill sets and personality types. Record a date by which you will transition these people out of leadership roles.

◻ What type of support is available for new leaders in your organization? What will you commit to providing as you look to better support those who are suddenly in charge?

12.

Corporate Pruning: Getting Rid of Dead Wood to Make Room for New Growth

Why do so many corporations choose to chop an entire forest of employees, rather than simply pruning back those employees who are clearly dead wood? Think about it. Everyone knows that these people are not working out. They are weighing the organization down. Yet nothing happens, until the company decides it's time to trim their workforce.

Leaders are stockpiling a lot of dead wood these days. Many managers fear that if they clear people out of the organization, they won't be able to find replacements. This fear is misguided.

When you fail to remove dead weight, you risk sinking the entire boat because the coworkers of underperforming employees will quickly tire from carrying an excess load. The employees who are able to pick up the slack are usually your most valuable players. These people will only be willing to stay for so long before they get fed up. When this happens, all that will remain are the average employees—and those who aren't making the grade.

Something else happens when you allow poor performers to remain in your employ. Coworkers go onto social media and sites like Glassdoor, and anonymously post about their experiences working in an organization filled with slackers. Trust me. These comments are *not* helping you as you look to seed your organization with new talent. I mean, think about it. Would you be chomping at the bit to apply for a job with a company that's filled with nonperformers? You might be, if you are a nonperformer yourself. However, my guess is you're not looking to hire more slackers. You want to attract and hire the best. This won't happen if current and former employees are calling out your company on social media.

Why Corporate Pruning Trumps Clear-cutting Every Time

The other day, my husband and I spent two hours wrestling with perennials that had infiltrated our garden. This wouldn't have happened if we had listened to the salesperson at the garden center, who advised us to cut these flowers back annually. My guess is this would have taken a grand total of ten minutes to do, had we done it every season. Our garden is now basically barren, and we'll need to start from zero come spring.

As I write this, I'm reminded of how corporations operate when it comes to pruning their workforces. When I read about a Fortune 500 company "downsizing" 100 people, I'm left thinking, "This isn't a downsizing, nor is it a reduction in force. This is a company that is getting rid of people they should have fired a long time ago!"

The problem with this workforce strategy is that when a "layoff" is announced, employee productivity comes to a halt—as does information sharing. Employees spend the majority of their work hours hoarding information, based on the belief that information is power. They operate under the assumption that if no one else knows what they know, then they'll be safe. I can't say I blame them. In many cases, they are right. The rest of their days are spent reconnecting with their network and going online to search for new jobs. One by one, employees start to bail, which signals to others that they should be doing the same. Before long, your workplace resembles my garden. It's barren.

Listen: Everyone makes hiring mistakes. What you do the moment you realize you've made a bad hire is what actually matters the most. Don't cling to a mistake just because you spent a lot of time making it. Prune as you go, and you won't be in the unenviable position of experiencing the chaos that ensues from deciding that today is the day to clean house.

Effective leaders constantly assess their workforce and make adjustments as they go along. They are not afraid to counsel and eliminate weak links because they know that pruning will allow other branches in the organization to thrive. As you assess the landscape of your organization, consider the following:

- What will happen if I do nothing?
- How much better off would we be if we got rid of those bad apples?
- Am I taking a risk that we will have to make drastic changes later if I don't take action now?
- Will my employees still blossom if I choose to do a layoff, rather than a termination?
- If I have to prune back the organization slightly, how do I make sure that I'm not cutting so deep that I kill innovation and customer service?

Determining Where and When to Cut

I'm often asked, "How do you know if it's time to cut your losses?" I usually answer this question with several questions of my own. I ask: "If you had to do it over again, would you make the same hiring decision?" If the answer is no, then either reassign this person to a position they're better suited for, or begin the process required to remove them from the organization. I'll also ask, "If you didn't need to involve HR or legal, would you fire this person?" A "Heck yes!" answer to this question is a strong indicator that this person needs to go.

In terms of when to cut, there is no such thing as an ideal time to let someone go. Of course, it's a good idea to avoid doing this around Thanksgiving or during the Christmas holidays. You don't want to be thoughtless or to cause undue financial strain in a terminated employee's life, especially at a time when most are gathering with family and friends. If an employee is relying on a scheduled Christmas bonus, you should let this person go long before the holiday. However, in terms of whether it's better to do this on a Friday or a Monday, in the morning or the afternoon, etc.—it no longer matters. The Internet is open twenty-four seven, giving terminated employees the opportunity to begin their job searches immediately.

Letting an employee go is never easy. Remember that the way you do this can have a lasting impact on both the employee, and the survivors. Approach this situation in a respectful manner. Be brief, communicate the reason for the termination, and offer whatever support you can to help your employee make a smooth transition. If you need a refresher on this, please revisit my "Timeless Tips for Tactful Termination," included in Chapter 7.

Maintaining a Stellar Employer Brand Throughout the Pruning Process

Most people understand that an organization may need to trim staff in order to remain viable. If you find yourself in this situation, be mindful of your approach. You don't want to wind up damaging your employer brand, which could take years to repair. Do the following and you should be fine:

Consider all options. At first glance, a reduction in force may seem like your only option. However, this may not be the case. Are some workers interested in reducing their hours? Are there opportunities for those who are able, to job share? Can you "loan" your employees to another organization that needs seasonal help? Hopefully by the time the next season comes around, you'll be in a better financial position to put these employees back to work.

Be generous. In all likelihood, you're making these cuts to save costs. However, the people who will be chopped are about to have their lives turned upside down. Consider how much you can afford to offer in severance pay. Then double that number. I can assure you that you could be spending a lot more money on attorney fees as people who feel wronged tend to lawyer up rather quickly. Extend employee benefits for as long as you can as it will take a while for people to figure out their next move, especially in terms of their health care.

Help people find their next opportunity. At the moment, there are plenty of jobs out there, which of course may not always be the case. Regardless of the state of the labor market, it will take time for people to find work. You can reduce the time it takes for your employees to find new employment by making a call on their behalf and introducing them to people in your network who may be hiring. This small act of generosity will go a long way toward helping those in need, and it might strengthen your employer brand as well.

Tending to the Rest of the Team

I've noticed that much more care and attention is spent on exiting employees than on those employees who are left remaining. Taking care of the people you will be terminating and those left behind is not a mutually exclusive endeavor. Take steps to ensure your team stays rooted—before, during, and after you prune.

BEFORE	DURING	AFTER
Share company financials with employees so they have a full understanding of the financial health of the organization.	If at all possible, avoid pulling groups of people into a conference room to inform them of the news. In situations like this, one-on-one conversations are best.	Reset the bar in terms of expectations going forward. Consider adjusting titles and pay for those taking on more responsibility as a result of the pruning.
Suggest to team members that they consider delaying major financial purchases until the organization is more stable.	Give employees a chance to say their goodbyes to their coworkers before escorting them out the door.	Be prepared for the exodus that may follow. Employees who highly value security may no longer wish to remain in your employ.
When responding to your employees' questions, be truthful. It's okay to say, "I don't know" or "I'm not at liberty to say."	Allow the remaining team members time to process the changes that have just occurred. Encourage them to come speak to you privately regarding any concerns they may have.	Hold regular meetings to keep employees in the loop regarding the organization's plans to get back on track.

Keep in mind that organizational changes are stressful for everyone, including yourself. Schedule time for self-care. You'll want to make sure you're mentally and physically in shape for the long road ahead, as you look to reengage your team.

Applying the Knowledge

As you think about areas that might need pruning to ensure your organization remains healthy, consider the following:

- Write down the name(s) of anyone in the organization that you consider dead weight.

- Add to this list the names of any employee whose behavior indicates they are no longer salvageable.

- Take note of those people who are doing jobs that can be absorbed by others, should you find that the cuts you'll need to make will be deep. Add their names to the list.

- Jot down a date next to the names of the people on your pruning list that indicates how soon you will take action.

- Write down what you'd like to ideally provide for those employees that are being let go. Work with your manager and your HR team to create a fair exit package.

- Write down questions you might be asked when rumors start flying about reductions in staff, along with how you will respond.

- Create a script that you will use to deliver the news that an employee's services are no longer needed. Practice your script in front of the mirror until you feel comfortable to deliver the news in person.

- Write down talking points that you want to include when you speak to those who are remaining on your team.

- ⌑ Examine your employee termination process. What, if anything, do you need to change to ensure people are treated with respect and compassion?

- ⌑ What one or two things can you do for yourself to reduce stress during this challenging time?

Conclusion:
Some Parting Words

I tend to buy way more than what I need when I make my annual trek to my local nursery. I chalk this up to all the excitement that I feel having survived another New England winter. As I look around the garden center, I see so many possibilities. As a result, I usually wind up wasting money on plants that don't fare well given my growing conditions. I also run out of steam about halfway through my planting frenzy, which leaves my poor husband to finish the work I started. In a nutshell, I bite off more than I can chew.

I don't want the same thing to happen to you. I've seeded this book with enough ideas to help you grow an evergreen forest of talent. Nevertheless, this is a fairly large task—especially if you have yet to even cultivate a small garden of talent. That's why I'm recommending that you pick one or two areas from each section of evergreen talent to focus on at first. Move these forward a mile, rather than attempt to move ten things forward an inch. Then pick a few more, until such time as you have a sustainable evergreen workforce.

Let me know how you're doing in terms of seeding, culti-vating, and growing your talent. Reach out to me at *Roberta@ MatusonConsulting.com* if I can be of help to you in any way.

Evergreen Talent Workbook

To plan out how you will seed, grow, and maintain evergreen tal-ent, download your *free* copy of the Evergreen Talent Workbook. It includes all the "Applying the Knowledge" questions in this book. You'll then have a customized Evergreen Talent Workbook for your organization.

What are you waiting for? Let's get growing! Download it for *free* at *www.MatusonConsulting.com/evergreentalent.*

Appendix

Here are some additional resources and tools to help you as you seed, grow, and cultivate evergreen talent. The following complimentary resources are available on our website, *www.MatusonConsulting.com,* in the section under "Resources." These resources will help you address those areas you've identified as needing attention.

- ¤ "Special Report: The Magnetic Organization: How to Attract Top Talent to Your Company"

- ¤ "Do You Want Some Dessert with That Turnover? Everything You Need to Calculate the *Real* Cost of Employee Turnover in Your Organization"

- ¤ "Thirty Low-Cost Ways to Show Your Employees They Are Highly Valued"

Roberta's Talent Maximizer: Sign up on our website (*www.MatusonConsulting.com*) to receive our complimentary newsletter. The newsletter is jammed packed with tips on employee retention, employee development, employee engagement, and productivity.

For more on this topic, be sure to check out Roberta's other books:

¤ *The Magnetic Leader* (Taylor and Francis, 2017)

¤ *Suddenly in Charge: Managing Up, Managing Down, Succeeding All Around* (Nicholas Brealey, 2017)

¤ *Talent Magnetism: How to Build a Workplace That Attracts and Keeps the Best* (Nicholas Brealey, 2013)

¤ *Selecting for Success: The Complete System for Hiring Top Talent,* by Roberta Matuson. Available for purchase on our website.

Notes

Chapter 1

1. Bureau of Labor Statistics News Release, Employment Projections 2016–2026, January 30, 2018.

Chapter 3

1. "Employee Engagement in US Stagnant in 2015," Gallup, *https://news.gallup.com*

2. "2016 Hiring Outlook: Strategies for Adapting to a Candidate-Driven Market," Execu/Search, *www.execu-search.com*

Chapter 4

1. Joseph B. Fuller and Manjari Raman, "Dismissed by Degrees: How Degree Inflation Is Undermining US Competitiveness and Hurting America's Middle Class," Harvard Business School, 2017.

2. US Department of Labor, "Job Openings and Labor Turnover," July 9, 2019, Bureau of Labor Statistics, *www.bls.gov*

3. "ZipRecruiter and the Call of Duty Endowment Release National Report on State of Veteran Employment Activity," Business Wire, November 9, 2017, *https://www.businesswire.com*

4. Department of Labor, July 2018.

Chapter 5

1. Steven F. Dichter, Chris Gagnon, and Ashok Alexander, "Leading Organizational Transformations," *McKinsey Quarterly,* February 1993.

2. Jobvite, 2015 Recruiter Nation, September, 2015.

Chapter 6

1. Christina Thompson, "10 Surprising Employee Engagement Statistics for 2018," *Quantum Workplace 2018 Employee Engagement Trends Report.*

2. *LinkedIn 2018 Workforce Learning Report.*

3. "US Employees' Willingness to Go Above and Beyond at Work Hits Three-Year Low, According to Gartner," September 11, 2018.

Chapter 8

1. Gallup Poll.

2. Execu/Search.

3. Ladders.

Chapter 11

1. TinyPulse.

Index

About the Author

For more than twenty-five years, Roberta Chinsky Matuson, president of Matuson Consulting, has helped leaders in highly regarded companies, including General Motors, New Balance, and Microsoft, and small to medium-size businesses, achieve dramatic growth and market leadership through the maximization of talent. She is known globally as The Talent Maximizer®.

Roberta is *the* person top employment site Monster and global retail giant Staples turn to for advice on talent. She is frequently quoted in the *Wall Street Journal,* the *New York Times,* and *Working Women* magazine. Roberta is the author of five books including *The Magnetic Leader* and the international bestseller *Suddenly in Charge,* a *Washington Post* Top 5 Business Book for Leaders. She is also an expert blogger for *Forbes* and *Thrive Global* and is a 2018 LinkedIn Top Voice in Management & Workplace.

Roberta is a Lynda.com/LinkedIn author whose work is heard by business executives at 40,000 feet, where she provides first-class advice in first-class cabins on Virgin, Emirates, and Turkish Airlines.

Roberta is one of a handful of people who have appeared as a guest of Bill O'Reilly's on Fox's *O'Reilly Factor,* and who left the show unscathed.

You can connect with the author at *www.MatusonConsulting.com.* Follow her on Twitter: *@matuson.* Connect with Roberta on LinkedIn.

Are you ready to plan and cultivate? Download the *free* companion *Evergreen Talent Workbook* at *www.MatusonConsulting. com/evergreentalent.*